THE LITTLE
CHUNKY
BOOK OF
DINOSAURS

The Little Chunky Book of Dinosaurs
Copyright © 2020 by Appleseed Press Book Publishers LLC.
This is an officially licensed book by Cider Mill Press Book Publishers LLC.

All rights reserved under the Pan-American and International Copyright Conventions.
No part of this book may be reproduced in whole or in part, scanned, photocopied, recorded,
distributed in any printed or electronic form, or reproduced in any manner whatsoever, or by any
information storage and retrieval system now known or hereafter invented, without express written
permission of the publisher, except in the case of brief quotations embodied in critical articles and
reviews.

The scanning, uploading, and distribution of this book via the Internet or via any other means
without permission of the publisher is illegal and punishable by law. Please support authors' rights,
and do not participate in or encourage piracy of copyrighted materials.

13-Digit ISBN: 978-1-60433-947-5
10-Digit ISBN: 1-60433-947-0

This book may be ordered by mail from the publisher. Please include $5.99 for postage and handling.
Please support your local bookseller first!

Books published by Cider Mill Press Book Publishers are available at special discounts for bulk
purchases in the United States by corporations, institutions, and other organizations.
For more information, please contact the publisher.

Cider Mill Press Book Publishers
"Where Good Books Are Ready for Press"
PO Box 454
12 Spring Street
Kennebunkport, Maine 04046
Visit us online!
cidermillpress.com

Typography: Block Berthold, Destroy, Gipsiero, Imperfect, PMN Caecilia
Image Credits: Images on pages 12–13, 16–17, 20, 22, 26–27, 32, 44–45, 54–55, 71, 75, 79, 82–83, 87, 91,
118–119, 125, 128–129, 132–133, 137, 140, 142–143, 148, 151, 158–159, 162–163, 168, 172–173, 176–177,
184–185, 192–193, 196–197, 200, 202–203, 208–209, 214–215, 218–219, 220–221, 226–227, 230–231, 242–243,
248–249, 252–253, 258–259, and 262–263 illustrated by Julius Csotonyi.
Images on pages 3, 36–37, 40, 96–97, 98–99, 104–105, 106–107, 154–155, 180–181, 188–189, and 204–205
illustrated by Bob and Tess Walters.
Image on pages 62–63 courtesy of Wikimedia Commons.
All other images and vectors used under official license from Shutterstock.com.

Printed in China
1 2 3 4 5 6 7 8 9 0
First Edition

THE LITTLE CHUNKY BOOK OF DINOSAURS

HUNDREDS of Fun Facts
Spanning MILLIONS of Years

INTRODUCTION

It's been millions of years since the last dinosaurs walked the Earth, but we are still as fascinated with these creatures as we've always been. Though we've only ever seen dinosaur bones, we recreate what they would look like in movies, on television, and in video games, and we travel to museums to learn about the different species. But what exactly were these creatures? How many of them were there? How long did they live? And why did they disappear?

True dinosaurs are a type of reptile that first appeared during the Triassic period. There are plenty of other prehistoric creatures (including ancient birds and mammals that we'll cover in this book as well), but true dinosaurs were always reptiles. There were hundreds of different families and species of dinosaurs, including carnivores (meat-eaters), herbivores (plant-eaters), and omnivores (meat- and plant-eaters). Dinosaurs are often separated into two major groups: *Saurischia* and *Ornithischia*. The biggest difference between the two had to do with the shape of their hips. *Saurischia*, or lizard-hipped dinosaurs, were usually carnivorous while the *Ornithischia*, or bird-hipped dinosaurs, were usually herbivorous.

Although dinosaurs first appeared in the Triassic period, different species were alive through the Cretaceous period. Although some species of dinosaurs may have naturally gone extinct, as some species do today, it's more likely that many species died out during what's called "mass extinctions." These mass extinctions were usually some kind of major event like a drastic change in climate that wiped out hundreds of species at the same time because they were no longer able to survive in their environment. By the end of the Cretaceous period (around 65 million years ago), no more true dinosaurs were alive, and most of their lineages had died out. We can't trace many modern animals back to dinosaurs, but there is some evidence that modern birds descended from dinosaurs!

So what's with all the wacky names? Most dinosaur names come from Latin or Greek, and they often describe something about the dinosaur. You can usually tell a true dinosaur because the first part of its name will end with "-*saurus*" or "-*saura*".

We can't see any true dinosaurs alive on the planet anymore, but we know they existed because we've discovered fossils. Fossils are naturally preserved pieces of evidence like bone fragments or footprints that can give scientists clues to how these creatures lived. Paleontologists are scientists who study fossils, but fossils are important to lots of other scientists, too. If you go to a museum, you might see giant dinosaur skeletons or fossils. Sometimes, museums have the original fossils. Other times, they make a mold or cast of the original fossil to put on display. It's very rare to discover complete dinosaur skeletons, so sometimes scientists have to fill in the missing bones based on similar species or what they think would have made sense.

Dinosaurs may not exist anymore, but they likely aren't going anywhere any time soon. These creatures are truly famous in popular culture, and it's unlikely we'll ever learn everything there is to know about them—but that doesn't mean we shouldn't keep trying to!

PREHISTORIC TIME LINE

PERMIAN PERIOD: 299 to 252 million years ago

TRIASSIC PERIOD: 252 to 201 million years ago

JURASSIC PERIOD: 201 to 145 million years ago

CRETACEOUS PERIOD: 145 to 66 million years ago

PALEOCENE EPOCH: 66 to 56 million years ago

EOCENE EPOCH: 56 to 33.9 million years ago

OLIGOCENE EPOCH: 33.9 to 23 million years ago

MIOCENE EPOCH: 23 to 5.3 million years ago

PLIOCENE EPOCH: 5.3 to 2.6 million years ago

PLEISTOCENE EPOCH: 2.6 to 0.01 million years ago

HOLOCENE EPOCH: 0.01 million years ago to present

DINO QUIZ

1. WHEN DID DINOSAURS BECOME EXTINCT?

A. 2 BILLION YEARS AGO

B. 7 MILLION YEARS AGO

C. 285 MILLION YEARS AGO

D. 65 MILLION YEARS AGO

2. WHAT ARE THE ONLY DINOSAUR RELATIVES THAT SURVIVED EXTINCTION?

A. FROGS

B. BIRDS

C. LIZARDS

D. SNAKES

3. WHEN DID DINOSAURS FIRST APPEAR?

A. JURASSIC PERIOD

B. CAMBRIAN PERIOD

C. CRETACEOUS PERIOD

D. TRIASSIC PERIOD

4. ALL TRUE DINOSAURS WERE . . .

A. BIRDS

B. FISH

C. REPTILES

D. MAMMALS

5. WHEN DID THE LAST TRUE DINOSAURS DIE OUT?

A. JURASSIC PERIOD

B. CRETACEOUS PERIOD

C. CAMBRIAN PERIOD

D. TRIASSIC PERIOD

ANSWERS: 1. D; 2. B; 3. D; 4. C; 5. B

PERMIAN PERIOD

299 TO 252 MILLION YEARS AGO

There may not have been any true dinosaurs alive during the **PERMIAN PERIOD**, but plenty of other fascinating creatures helped pave the way for dinosaurs. When the Permian period started, it's likely that Earth was just coming out of an ice age. As the ice melted, sea levels rose, and the continents started to spread. A great number of animals started to roam the planet. During the Permian period, the continents as we know them today would have been pushed together in one massive landform known as Pangaea. The sea levels were much lower than they are now, and many of the most prominent creatures were land animals. The end of the Permian period was marked by what was likely the worst mass extinction ever, killing most of the aquatic species (species that lived in the water) and about 75 percent of the terrestrial species (species that lived on land).

DIMETRODON LIMBATUS

PRONUNCIATION: DY-met-RO-don

SIZE: Up to 15 feet (4.6 meters) long

LIVED: 295 to 272 million years ago

PHYSICAL PROFILE: A squat, four-legged carnivore that sported a huge, thin sail along its back

This reptilian species may look like a dinosaur, but it's technically not one. Scientists suspect that *Dimetrodon* was warm-blooded, while dinosaurs were cold-blooded reptiles.

Even though *Dimetrodon* was a warm-blooded creature, it still reproduced by laying eggs like most reptiles.

DIMETRODON WOULD NEVER HAVE MET ANY DINOSAURS. IN FACT, DIMETRODON WAS LIKELY EXTINCT ABOUT 40 MILLION YEARS BEFORE THE FIRST DINOSAURS EXISTED!

PICTURE A SAIL ON A SAILBOAT—DIMETRODON HAD A HUGE SAIL MADE OF SPINES AND SKIN ON ITS BACK!

Other species of prehistoric creatures had similar sails to *Dimetrodon*, but it is the first known species with this trait.

DESPITE THE NAME, *DIMETRODON* DIDN'T USE ITS SAIL TO CATCH THE WIND! PALEONTOLOGISTS ONCE THOUGHT THAT *DIMETRODON* USED ITS SAIL TO REGULATE TEMPERATURE, HELPING IT TO WARM UP OR COOL DOWN.

Newer evidence suggests the giant sail was all for show. It may have been what's called a "display structure," which would have helped this predator to spot other *Dimetrodon* as it walked across the Permian landscape.

ANOTHER THEORY IS THAT THE SAIL WAS A WAY TO SHOW OFF DURING THE MATING SEASON, LIKE A BIG BILLBOARD SHOWING HOW STRONG AND COLORFUL *DIMETRODON* WAS.

It wasn't just adults that had sails. Baby *Dimetrodon* had tiny sails on their backs, just like their parents!

THIS WELL-DECORATED PREDATOR WAS LIKELY AT THE TOP OF THE FOOD CHAIN. *DIMETRODON* WOULD HAVE EATEN FISH AS WELL AS OTHER REPTILES AND AMPHIBIANS.

Dimetrodon teeth were pretty frightening. Some of them had serrated edges like a saw, helping this carnivore chomp down on prey.

DINOGORGON RUBIDGEI
PRONUNCIATION: DY-no-GORE-gon

SIZE: About 6 feet (2 meters) long

LIVED: 252 million years ago

PHYSICAL PROFILE: A hunter that ran on all fours and dispatched prey with long, pointed canine teeth

Dinogorgon technically wasn't a dinosaur, but it was one of the last great predatory protomammals, which means that it was a warm-blooded reptile.

THE FIRST *DINOGORGON* FOSSILS WERE FOUND IN THE 1930S OR 1940S ON A FARM IN SOUTH AFRICA.

Because of the fossil locations, scientists think *Dinogorgon* likely lived in what's now South Africa and Tanzania.

The name *Dinogorgon* translates to "terrible gorgon." Gorgons were creatures in Greek mythology that had snakes for hair.

CAN YOU IMAGINE TONS OF SPECIES GOING EXTINCT AT THE SAME TIME? THAT'S EXACTLY WHAT HAPPENED AT THE END OF THE PERMIAN PERIOD, AND *DINOGORGON* WAS ONE OF MANY SPECIES WIPED OUT IN A MASS EXTINCTION.

DINOGORGON COULD GROW TO BE 6.5 FEET (2 METERS) LONG, OR ABOUT THE SIZE OF A BLACK BEAR.

What large teeth you have, *Dinogorgon!* Long saber teeth made *Dinogorgon* one of the fiercest predators of the Permian period.

HEY *DINOGORGON*, WHAT'S FOR DINNER? THIS PREHISTORIC PREDATOR HUNTED OTHER REPTILES AND SMALLER ANIMALS.

Long teeth weren't the only weapons *Dinogorgon* had at its disposal. *Dinogorgon* was also much faster than earlier Permian predators.

ITS SPEED WAS LIKELY DUE TO ITS BODY SHAPE. WHILE OTHER CREATURES OF THE TIME HAD LEGS SPLAYED OUT TO THE SIDE, *DINOGORGON* HAD LEGS THAT WERE MORE UPRIGHT AND CLOSER TO THE MIDDLE OF ITS BODY. THIS POSITION LET IT MOVE AROUND QUICKLY.

TITANOSUCHUS FEROX

PRONUNCIATION: TIE-tan-O-sook-US

SIZE: Up to 9 feet (2.75 meters) long

LIVED: About 265 million years ago

PHYSICAL PROFILE: A protomammal that walked on four legs and had a long skull full of pointed teeth that differed in shape from front to back

LIKE OTHER CREATURES IN THE PERMIAN PERIOD, *TITANOSUCHUS* WAS A WARM-BLOODED REPTILE KNOWN AS A PROTOMAMMAL.

Have you heard the word "titan" before? Titans were creatures in Greek mythology known for their massive size and impressive strength, just like *Titanosuchus*.

***TITANOSUCHUS* LIKELY LIVED IN MODERN-DAY SOUTH AFRICA, WHERE FOSSILS HAVE BEEN FOUND.**

Does *Titanosuchus* look like any modern animals to you? Its name "-*suchus*" is a reference to its crocodile-like body. The same name is even used to describe modern crocodiles—the West African crocodile has the scientific name *Crocodylus suchus*.

MOST REPTILES HAVE SCALY SKIN, BUT NOT *TITANOSUCHUS*. INSTEAD, *TITANOSUCHUS* HAD SMOOTH SKIN THAT MAY HAVE BEEN PARTLY COVERED IN HAIR.

Titanosuchus was closely related to *Moschops capensis* (see page 22), another protomammal, but these relatives were far from friendly. *Titanosuchus* was a fierce predator that would hunt *Moschops* as prey.

JONKERIA TRUCULENTA (SEE PAGE 24), ANOTHER CLOSE RELATIVE, MAY ALSO HAVE BEEN PREY FOR *TITANOSUCHUS*.

How could *Titanosuchus* hunt such large prey? It was no small creature and could grow up to around 8 feet (2.4 meters) long.

TITANOSUCHUS HAD SHARP INCISORS AND FANGLIKE CANINE TEETH, WHICH HELPED IT TO CHOMP DOWN ON ITS PREY AND PROVIDED A HUGE ADVANTAGE FOR THESE PREHISTORIC HUNTERS.

MOSCHOPS CAPENSIS

PRONUNCIATION: Moe-shops

SIZE: Up to 9 feet (2.75 meters) long

LIVED: About 265 million years ago

PHYSICAL PROFILE: This heavily built protomammal had a unique, domed head.

The name *Moschops* comes from the Greek for "calf face."

LIKE OTHER PROTOMAMMALS, *MOSCHOPS* FOSSILS HAVE BEEN FOUND IN SOUTH AFRICA.

This herbivore wasn't a predator, but it did fight by butting heads, which may have been the reason for its short, thick, skull.

EVER HEARD THE TERM "THICKHEADED"? *MOSCHOPS* HAD A DOMED HEAD THAT WAS INCREDIBLY UNIQUE AND REINFORCED WITH DENSE BONE THAT WAS MUCH THICKER THAN OTHER ANIMALS ALIVE AT THE TIME.

Moschops was one of the largest protomammals. It had elbowlike joints that would have helped it to walk much like modern-day mammals do.

THIS HEAVY ANIMAL LIKELY MOVED PRETTY SLOWLY THANKS TO ITS MASSIVE BUILD.

Because *Moschops* wasn't a fast runner, it would have relied on its large size to protect itself from predators.

THOUGH THEY SOMETIMES COMPETED WITH EACH OTHER, SCIENTISTS ALSO THINK *MOSCHOPS* MAY HAVE MOVED IN HERDS OR SMALL GROUPS.

Although the name might conjure images of cattle, this creature was somewhat closer to a hippopotamus because it may have lived partially in the water.

JONKERIA TRUCULENTA

PRONUNCIATION: Yon-keh-ree-ah

Although many scientists believe *Jonkeria* was an herbivore, some suspect it may have been an omnivore, which means it would eat both plants and meat.

SIZE: About 12 feet (over 3.6 meters) long

LIVED: About 265 million years ago

PHYSICAL PROFILE: *Jonkeria* was a large, heavy protomammal with an extremely long snout.

THEIR HEADS AREN'T THE ONLY SIMILAR THINGS BETWEEN *TITANOSUCHUS FEROX* (SEE PAGE 20) AND *JONKERIA*. THEY ALSO LIVED AROUND THE SAME TIME AND IN THE SAME REGION, SO THEY LIKELY WOULD HAVE CROSSED PATHS. *TITANOSUCHUS* MAY HAVE EVEN HUNTED *JONKERIA*.

Although *Jonkeria truculenta* may have been the most common species, there are about a dozen different species within the *Jonkeria* family.

The snout of *Jonkeria* looks incredibly similar to the snout of *Titanosuchus* because of the proportions. It's twice as long as it is wide.

Though their heads were similar, *Jonkeria* had much shorter limbs on their bulky bodies than *Titanosuchus*.

Eating meat doesn't necessarily make *Jonkeria* a hunter. Its massive size means it could have been a meat eater of opportunity by scaring off smaller predators and claiming their prey.

Jonkeria had large incisor and canine teeth, which would have let it eat tougher food than just plants. This makes scientists think it could have eaten meat.

ARCHOSAURUS ROSSICUS
PRONUNCIATION: ARK-uh-SAWR-us

SIZE: About 10 feet (3 meters) long

LIVED: Around 252 million years ago

PHYSICAL PROFILE: *Archosaurus* hunted prey on all fours and had a downward-angled snout that gave it a snaggletoothed look.

Archosaurus was one of the largest reptilian predators of the Permian period, setting the stage for its relatives to become even bigger during the Triassic period.

Archosaurus fossils have mostly been found in Russia, and the species was first described in 1960.

Archosaurus skulls alone were huge, measuring just over 1 foot (0.3 meter) long.

This predator had sharp, long teeth and a unique hooked upper jaw shape that would have helped it to hold onto its prey.

TRUE OR FALSE

1. T / F THE CONTINENTS AS WE KNOW THEM TODAY WERE ALL CLUMPED TOGETHER AS ONE MASSIVE LANDFORM CALLED PANGAEA.

2. T / F *TITANOSUCHUS FEROX* WAS COVERED IN SCALY SKIN.

3. T / F *DIMETRODON LIMBATUS* LIVED AT THE SAME TIME AS DINOSAURS.

4. T/F **ARCHOSAURUS ROSSICUS WAS ONE OF THE SMALLEST REPTILIAN PREDATORS DURING THE PERMIAN PERIOD.**

5. T/F **MOSCHOPS CAPENSIS WAS PART OF A GROUP OF ANIMALS KNOWN AS PROTOMAMMALS, WHICH MEANS IT WAS A WARM-BLOODED REPTILE.**

ANSWERS: 1. T; 2. F; 3. F; 4. F; 5. T

TRIASSIC PERIOD

252 TO 201 MILLION YEARS AGO

Sometimes, tragedy makes way for success. In the wake of the worst mass extinction of all time at the end of the Permian period, most of the creatures that had formerly ruled the food chain had disappeared. This opened the door for new species to grow and develop.

The continents were still combined in the landmass called Pangaea, and the landscape was dry and desertlike. But about halfway through this time period, the climate started to turn more humid and the landmass split into two different areas. Laurasia moved north, while Gondwana moved south. The first of the dinosaurs evolved during the Triassic period, but they weren't much like the top-of-the-food-chain predators we often picture. Triassic dinosaurs were still adapting, changing, and learning the ropes to help them make their way to the top.

EORAPTOR LUNENSIS
PRONUNCIATION: EE-o-RAP-tor

SIZE: About 3 feet (1 meter) long

LIVED: About 231 million years ago

PHYSICAL PROFILE: One of the earliest known dinosaurs, *Eoraptor* was a bipedal animal with leaf-shaped teeth.

The name "*Eoraptor*" means "dawn thief," because this predator was one of the first dinosaurs that lived during the "dawn" of the age of dinosaurs.

The second part of its name, "*lunensis*", means "of the moon." This might sound like the opposite of the dawn, but it's actually a reference to the park in Argentina where Eoraptor fossils were first found, which is called the Valley of the Moon.

EORAPTOR FOSSILS HAVE BEEN FOUND IN PRESENT-DAY ARGENTINA AND MADAGASCAR.

One fossil found in Argentina in 1991 was actually an *Eoraptor* skull! The discovery of the skull in a rock was a major find considering how old this dinosaur was, and scientists have been able to locate almost three complete *Eoraptor* skeletons.

DON'T LET ITS SMALL SIZE FOOL YOU. *EORAPTOR* WAS A FAST, FEROCIOUS HUNTER THAT WAS LIKELY AN ANCESTOR TO OTHER PREDATORY DINOSAURS.

This dinosaur had a light skull and bones and likely weighed about 20 pounds (9 kilograms).

ALTHOUGH SCIENTISTS HAVE BEEN ABLE TO STUDY A FEW SKULLS, THE ONES THEY'VE FOUND HAD BONES THAT WEREN'T FUSED AND EYE SOCKETS THAT WERE VERY LARGE COMPARED TO THE REST OF THE SKULL. THESE TWO TRAITS ARE COMMON IN YOUNG SKULLS, WHICH HAS LED SCIENTISTS TO THINK THAT THEY MAY NOT HAVE FOUND ANY ADULT REMAINS YET.

Underneath those skulls, *Eoraptor* also had a noticeably large neck compared to other dinosaurs at the time.

HAVE YOU EVER PICTURED A DINOSAUR WITH HANDS? *EORAPTOR* HAD SHORT, GRASPING HANDS WITH FIVE FINGERS THAT IT COULD USE TO GRAB ONTO PREY.

Although *Eoraptor* had five fingers, scientists suspect that only about three of them were really effective for grabbing. The other two stubby fingers weren't very useful. That might explain why later species of dinosaurs had fewer fingers.

Though it may have used its shorter limbs to walk on all fours, *Eoraptor* more likely spent its time walking on two feet.

EORAPTOR LIVED ALONGSIDE THE LARGER, SHARP-TOOTHED *HERRERASAURUS ISCHIGUALASTENSIS* (SEE PAGE 36), WHICH COULD GROW UP TO 20 FEET (6 METERS) LONG, AND SCIENTISTS THINK *HERRERASAURUS* MAY HAVE EVEN HUNTED *EORAPTOR*.

The small and agile predator *Eodromaeus murphi* (see page 40) also lived and hunted alongside *Eoraptor*.

EORAPTOR HAD A VARIETY OF DIFFERENT-SHAPED TEETH, INCLUDING ONES THAT LOOKED LIKE BLADES AND ONES THAT LOOKED LIKE LEAVES. THIS MAY HAVE ALLOWED IT TO EAT BOTH PLANTS AND MEAT, MAKING THIS DINOSAUR AN OMNIVORE.

HERRERASAURUS ISCHIGUALASTENSIS

PRONUNCIATION: Heh-RARE-uh-SORE-us

If evolution were a race, *Herrerasaurus* would win first place! *Herrerasaurus* may have been one of the first true dinosaurs to walk the Earth.

HUMANS HAVE FIVE TOES ON EACH FOOT, AND SO DID *HERRERASAURUS!* EACH OF ITS FEET HAD FIVE TOES, BUT SCIENTISTS THINK THAT ONLY THE THREE MIDDLE TOES WERE VERY USEFUL IN BEARING THIS DINOSAUR'S WEIGHT.

SIZE: About 20 feet (6 meters) long

LIVED: About 231 million years ago

PHYSICAL PROFILE: A predator with a long, narrow skull, a long tail, and strong legs with long feet

WITH ITS STRONG BACK LEGS, HERRERASAURUS WOULD HAVE BEEN ENTIRELY BIPEDAL, MEANING IT WALKED ON TWO LEGS INSTEAD OF FOUR.

Because of its specialized back legs and toes, *Herrerasaurus* was likely a fast runner.

HERRERASAURUS HAD SHORT ARMS THAT WERE ABOUT HALF THE SIZE OF ITS LEGS.

Each of those short arms also had five fingers, but only the first three were clawed fingers that would have been useful in catching prey.

HOW DO SCIENTISTS KNOW HERRERASAURUS WAS THE FIRST TRUE DINOSAUR? THE LEG AND ARM ANATOMY OF HERRERASAURUS ARE THE MAIN REASONS SCIENTISTS THINK THIS CREATURE MAY HAVE BEEN ONE OF THE FIRST DINOSAURS.

Herrerasaurus was no small animal. It could weigh up to 700 pounds (317.5 kilograms)!

ITS LONG, THICK TAIL WOULD HAVE HELPED HERRERASAURUS TO BALANCE OUT ITS WEIGHT.

You wouldn't want to get caught in this creature's jaws. *Herrerasaurus* had a long, narrow skull that was filled with dozens of sharp teeth.

BECAUSE OF THE SERRATED SHAPE OF ITS TEETH AND ITS CLAWS, IT'S LIKELY THAT *HERRERASAURUS* WAS A CARNIVORE. IT WOULD HAVE PREYED ON SMALLER CREATURES LIKE *PISANOSAURUS MERTII* (PAGE 42).

Being a carnivore didn't mean this dinosaur was safe from danger. In fact, it was likely hunted by the larger *Postosuchus kirkpatricki* (see page 45) and *Sarcosuchus imperator*.

FOSSILS OF *HERRERASAURUS* HAVE BEEN FOUND IN SOUTH AMERICA, ESPECIALLY IN ARGENTINA.

An Argentinian goat herder named Victorino Herrera found the first fossils of *Herrerasaurus* by accident.

You might have already guessed it, but *Herrerasaurus* actually means "Herrera's lizard," as this dinosaur was named after the man who first discovered it.

EODROMAEUS MURPHI
PRONUNCIATION: EE-oh-DRO-may-US

SIZE: About 4 feet (1.2 meters) long

LIVED: About 230 million years ago

PHYSICAL PROFILE: A small predator, *Eodromaeus* had two short arms and two longer hind legs.

Eodromaeus had sharp teeth that were different from the leaf-shaped teeth of *Eoraptor lunensis* (see page 32).

The name *Eodromaeus* means "dawn runner," because this animal was thought to be one of the first dinosaurs at the "dawn" of the age of dinosaurs.

If you take a trip to Argentina, you'll be able to get a rough picture of where *Eodromaeus* lived. Fossils from two different *Eodromaeus* have been found in modern-day Argentina.

Do you have a sibling that looks a lot like you? Because of physical similarities, scientists first thought that *Eodromaeus* fossils were *Eoraptor lunensis*.

AS SCIENTISTS LOOKED CLOSER AT THE FOSSILS OF *EODROMAEUS*, THEY DISCOVERED DIFFERENCES THAT MADE IT CLEAR THIS WAS NO *EORAPTOR*, BUT THE TWO ARE CLOSELY RELATED.

Eodromaeus also had grasping fingers, much like *Eoraptor*.

Later dinosaurs are known for having three fingers, and although *Eodromaeus* had five, the last two fingers were much smaller and likely weren't used much. This trait helped explain to scientists why later dinosaurs had fewer fingers.

This small creature was a carnivore, and it would have used its fingers, teeth, and speed to catch prey.

THIS LIGHT DINOSAUR LIKELY ONLY WEIGHED ABOUT 11 POUNDS (5 KILOGRAMS).

MUCH LIKE *EORAPTOR*, *EODROMAEUS* HAD STRONG BACK LEGS AND LIKELY WALKED UPRIGHT.

PISANOSAURUS MERTII

PRONUNCIATION: Pie-SAN-o-SORE-us

EVEN SCIENTISTS ARE CONFUSED BY THIS MYSTERIOUS CREATURE! ALTHOUGH *PISANOSAURUS* WAS ORIGINALLY CLASSIFIED AS A DINOSAUR, SCIENTISTS NOW AREN'T SURE WHETHER THAT CLASSIFICATION IS CORRECT. INSTEAD, THEY THINK *PISANOSAURUS* MAY HAVE BEEN A VERY CLOSE RELATIVE TO OTHER TYPES OF DINOSAURS.

SIZE: About 3 feet (1 meter) long

LIVED: Between 228 and 216 million years ago

PHYSICAL PROFILE: A small, lightly built herbivore

Fossils of this small creature were first discovered in modern-day Argentina. Not many remains have been found, which means that there is still a lot to learn about this animal.

Because of its ridged teeth, *Pisanosaurus* was likely an herbivore.

Danger was everywhere for the prehistoric *Pisanosaurus*. It would have lived in the same time and habitat as the predatory *Herrerasaurus ischigualastensis* (see page 36).

This light lizard would have weighed somewhere between 5 to 20 pounds (2.3 to 9 kilograms).

Scientists think *Pisanosaurus* was bipedal, but how do they know? The shoulder blades and forearm of *Pisanosaurus* were small, which could mean that it walked on two legs rather than four.

The name *Pisanosaurus* means "Pisano's lizard," and this animal was named to honor Juan Arnaldo Pisano, an Argentinian paleontologist.

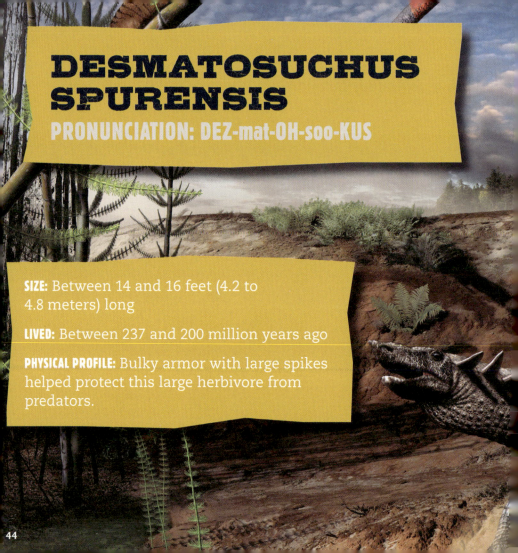

DESMATOSUCHUS SPURENSIS

PRONUNCIATION: DEZ-mat-OH-soo-KUS

SIZE: Between 14 and 16 feet (4.2 to 4.8 meters) long

LIVED: Between 237 and 200 million years ago

PHYSICAL PROFILE: Bulky armor with large spikes helped protect this large herbivore from predators.

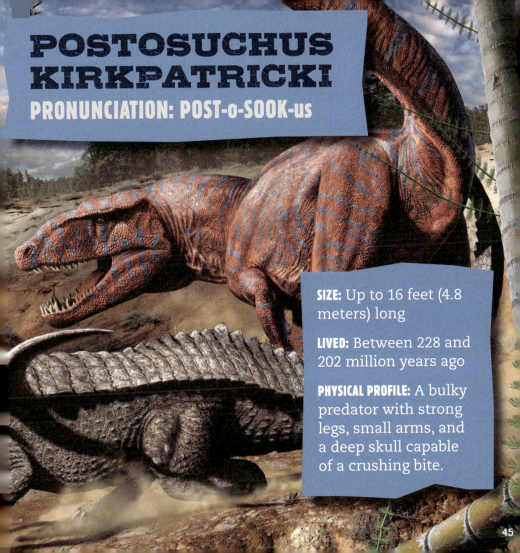

POSTOSUCHUS KIRKPATRICKI
PRONUNCIATION: POST-o-SOOK-us

SIZE: Up to 16 feet (4.8 meters) long

LIVED: Between 228 and 202 million years ago

PHYSICAL PROFILE: A bulky predator with strong legs, small arms, and a deep skull capable of a crushing bite.

DESMATOSUCHUS SPURENSIS

The teeth say it all. *Desmatosuchus* had blunt teeth that indicate it was an herbivore.

HAVE YOU EVER SEEN A KNIGHT WEARING BODY ARMOR FOR PROTECTION? DESPITE NOT BEING A PREDATOR, THIS HERBIVORE'S BODY ARMOR CERTAINLY GAVE IT A FIGHTING CHANCE.

Plates and spikes all along *Desmatosuchus's* back would have been made of bone embedded in its skin. These are called osteoderms, meaning "skin bones."

Paleontologists have found some relatives of *Desmatosuchus* with parts of their armor still in place after more than 220 million years.

ALTHOUGH THE ARMOR WOULD HAVE PROTECTED ITS BODY, DESMATOSUCHUS WAS CERTAINLY STILL IN DANGER BECAUSE ITS HEAD WAS EXPOSED TO ATTACKS.

Does this creature look familiar? *Desmatosuchus* was closely related to modern crocodiles.

With its low body and short legs, *Desmatosuchus* walked on all fours.

Desmatosuchus may have lived and looked for food in the mud near bodies of water.

FOSSILS FROM A FEW DIFFERENT *DESMATOSUCHUS* HAVE BEEN FOUND IN MODERN-DAY TEXAS.

Humans use shovels to dig up the ground, but *Desmatosuchus* had a built-in shovel! *Desmatosuchus* had a shovel-like snout that scientists think may have helped it to dig for food.

Although it most likely ate vegetation, some scientists think *Desmatosuchus* could also have eaten insects because its snout is shaped like modern armadillos'. This would make it an omnivore rather than a true herbivore, but most scientists don't think it's very likely.

POSTOSUCHUS KIRKPATRICKI

Because of its strong legs and comparatively small arms, scientists suspect that *Postosuchus* was a bipedal creature, which means it would have walked on two legs.

Within its deep skull, *Postosuchus* had daggerlike teeth that it would have used to hunt other, smaller creatures.

Along with its teeth, *Postosuchus* would have used its long, curved claws to catch prey.

POSTOSUCHUS LOOKS LIKE A DINOSAUR WITH ITS KNIFE-LIKE TEETH AND ABILITY TO WALK ON TWO LEGS, BUT IT WAS ACTUALLY A CLOSER RELATIVE TO THE EARLIEST CROCODILES.

Scientists know *Postosuchus* wasn't a true dinosaur because of the anatomy of its hips and ankles.

During a time when dinosaurs were rare and small, crocodile cousins like *Postosuchus* were the true rulers of the Triassic world.

Damaged armor plates found in Triassic rock suggest that predators like *Postosuchus* were capable of literally cracking the defenses of their victims.

THE NAME *POSTOSUCHUS* MEANS "CROCODILE FROM POST," WHICH REFERS TO AN AREA IN MODERN-DAY TEXAS CALLED POST QUARRY WHERE A NUMBER OF *POSTOSUCHUS* FOSSILS WERE FOUND.

Postosuchus had rows of protective plates along its back that would have helped it defend itself.

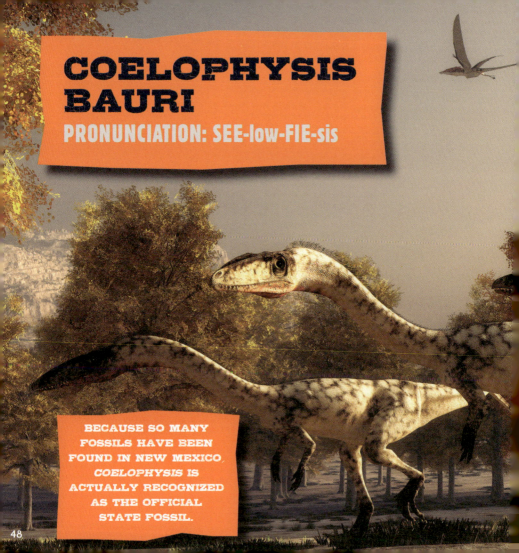

COELOPHYSIS BAURI
PRONUNCIATION: SEE-low-FIE-sis

BECAUSE SO MANY FOSSILS HAVE BEEN FOUND IN NEW MEXICO, *COELOPHYSIS* IS ACTUALLY RECOGNIZED AS THE OFFICIAL STATE FOSSIL.

SIZE: Between 6 and 9 feet (1.8 and 2.74 meters) long

LIVED: Between 228 and 200 million years ago

PHYSICAL PROFILE: A small carnivore with a slender neck, *Coelophysis* had a long, narrow jaw with plenty of sharp teeth to help it catch prey.

Have you ever wanted to go to space? *Coelophysis* actually did! The skull of *Coelophysis* was on board the Space Shuttle *Endeavour* mission STS-89, which launched into space on January 22, 1998.

Coelophysis fossils have been discovered in Africa and North America.

This small carnivore was by no means top of the food chain. During the late Triassic, larger creatures like *Postosuchus kirkpatricki* (see page 45) were much higher up on the food chain.

THIS PREDATOR WAS MUCH SMALLER THAN OTHERS OF THE TIME AND WOULD ONLY HAVE WEIGHED AROUND 50 POUNDS (22.6 KILOGRAMS).

That light weight was a result of hollow bones. Those bones gave *Coelophysis* its name, which means "hollow form."

The light build would have helped *Coelophysis* to be a quick, agile hunter.

Coelophysis had sharp teeth and grasping claws, which would have helped this carnivore to catch prey.

Each arm had four fingers, but only three were functional for grasping. The fourth was much smaller and not as useful.

HAVE YOU EVER SPLIT APART A WISHBONE? *COELOPHYSIS* ACTUALLY HAD A WISHBONE. IT WAS LIKELY THE FIRST DINOSAUR WITH THIS TRAIT.

The presence of a wishbone and hollow bones are both traits of modern-day birds, showing that *Coelophysis* may have been a very early bird ancestor.

By studying the shape of its long, narrow head, scientists have learned that *Coelophysis* likely had excellent vision and great depth perception, which would have been very useful as a hunter.

COELOPHYSIS WALKED ON TWO LEGS AND WAS PROBABLY A PRETTY FAST RUNNER.

Like other predators, *Coelophysis* had bladelike, sharp, serrated teeth that would have helped it catch prey.

Coelophysis likely hunted other small, lizard-like animals.

SOME SCIENTISTS USED TO THINK THAT *COELOPHYSIS* WOULD EAT OTHER *COELOPHYSIS* BECAUSE OF THE DISCOVERY OF ONE FOSSIL THAT APPEARED TO HAVE REMAINS IN ITS STOMACH OF ANOTHER *COELOPHYSIS*. LATER, SCIENTISTS FOUND THAT THE REMAINS IN THE STOMACH WERE LIKELY NOT *COELOPHYSIS* AT ALL, BUT A CROCODILE-LIKE CREATURE.

Scientists think that *Coelophysis* may have hunted in packs at times.

THIS THEORY COMES FROM THE FACT THAT FOSSILS FROM MANY DIFFERENT *COELOPHYSIS* HAVE BEEN DISCOVERED IN THE SAME PLACE.

In fact, one fossil site in Ghost Ranch, New Mexico, had fossils that may have belonged to up to 1,000 different *Coelophysis*.

One theory as to why so many *Coelophysis* were found in the same place is that a flash flood suddenly killed and buried them.

DINO QUIZ

1. WHAT MODERN ANIMAL DOES *POSTOSUCHUS KIRKPATRICKI* MOST RESEMBLE?

A. ELEPHANT

B. SNAKE

C. CROCODILE

D. WHALE

2. WHAT DID THE NAME "*EODROMAEUS MURPHI*" MEAN?

A. DAWN RUNNER

B. NIGHT RUNNER

C. DAWN THIEF

D. NIGHT THIEF

3. **WHICH DINOSAUR WAS THE FIRST TO HAVE A WISHBONE?**

A. *HERRERASAURUS ISCHIGUALASTENSIS*

B. *COELOPHYSIS BAURI*

C. *DESMATOSUCHUS SPURENSIS*

D. *POSTOSUCHUS KIRKPATRICKI*

4. **HOW BIG WAS *EORAPTOR LUNENSIS*?**

A. 3 FEET (1 METER) LONG

B. 5 FEET (1.5 METERS) LONG

C. 7 FEET (ABOUT 2 METERS) LONG

D. 10 FEET (3 METERS) LONG

5. **WHAT TYPE OF EATER WAS *PISANOSAURUS MERTII*?**

A. CARNIVORE

B. OMNIVORE

C. HERBIVORE

Answers: 1. C; 2. A; 3. B; 4. A; 5. C

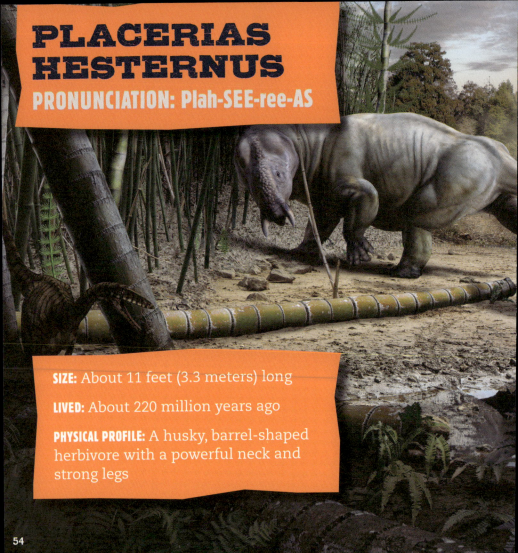

PLACERIAS HESTERNUS

PRONUNCIATION: Plah-SEE-ree-AS

SIZE: About 11 feet (3.3 meters) long

LIVED: About 220 million years ago

PHYSICAL PROFILE: A husky, barrel-shaped herbivore with a powerful neck and strong legs

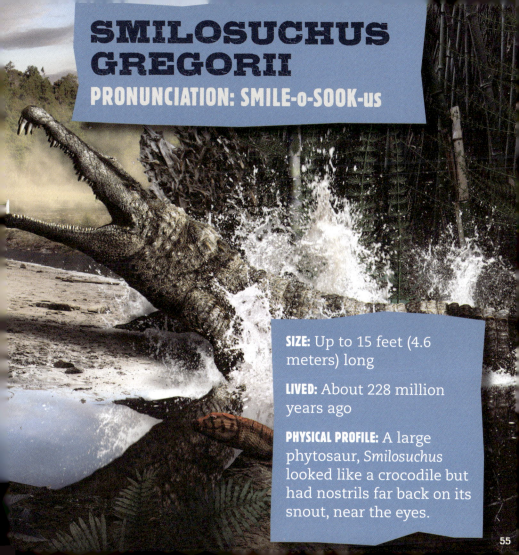

SMILOSUCHUS GREGORII

PRONUNCIATION: SMILE-o-SOOK-us

SIZE: Up to 15 feet (4.6 meters) long

LIVED: About 228 million years ago

PHYSICAL PROFILE: A large phytosaur, *Smilosuchus* looked like a crocodile but had nostrils far back on its snout, near the eyes.

PLACERIAS HESTERNUS

The *Placerias* was one of the largest herbivores of the Triassic and could weigh up to 2,000 pounds (907 kilograms).

A TUSKED, TUBBY HERBIVORE, PLACERIAS WAS ONE OF THE LAST SURVIVING MEMBERS OF PROTOMAMMALS CALLED DICYNODONTS. THESE BEAKED PLANT-EATERS WERE FREQUENTLY FOOD FOR THE CARNIVORES THEY LIVED ALONGSIDE.

Thanks to some bitten Triassic bones, paleontologists know that phytosaurs sometimes ate protomammals such as the unlucky *Placerias*.

The name *Placerias* means "broad body," and it's certainly fitting given this animal's massive size.

FOSSILS OF OVER 30 DIFFERENT *PLACERIAS* WERE FOUND IN ARIZONA IN THE 1930S.

So many fossils grouped together suggest that *Placerias* may have traveled in herds.

Placerias would have walked on all fours on its short, squat legs.

Does *Placerias* remind you at all of a hippopotamus? There might be a good reason for that similarity. Scientists think *Placerias* may have submerged itself in water.

Placerias didn't just go in the water to take a swim. Hiding in the water may have been a way for it to avoid predatory land animals.

WITH ITS SHORT TUSKS, *PLACERIAS* WAS LIKELY AN HERBIVORE. IT MOST LIKELY FED ON GRASS NEAR LAKES AND RIVERS.

Those tusks may have been there as a form of protection, helping *Placerias* fight off its attackers.

SMILOSUCHUS GREGORII

The most common carnivores of the Triassic period were phytosaurs like *Smilosuchus*.

Smilosuchus may look a lot like modern crocodiles, but one way to tell the difference between the two is by looking at the placement of their nostrils—phytosaurs had nostrils on the tops of their skulls, near the eyes, rather than at the front like crocodiles.

SMILOSUCHUS WOULD HAVE ACTED A LOT LIKE MODERN CROCODILES, LAUNCHING AT PREY FROM THE WATER'S EDGE.

This carnivore was dangerous, and along with the likes of *Postosuchus kirkpatricki* (see page 45) and early dinosaurs, they made the Triassic period a very dangerous time to be alive.

Even the best hunters miss sometimes. *Smilosuchus* wasn't always successful in catching prey. Paleontologists have found a leg bone of another Triassic predator with phytosaur tooth marks surrounded by healed bone, meaning the animal escaped a close call with a carnivore like *Smilosuchus*.

SMILOSUCHUS WOULD HAVE BEEN COMFORTABLE IN THE WATER OR ON LAND.

With its long, powerful tail and short legs, *Smilosuchus* likely moved on all fours.

Smilosuchus had large, bladelike teeth at the back of its mouth that would have been able to easily slice into prey.

Because it was such a large, fierce predator, *Smilosuchus* would have been able to hunt dinosaurs like *Placerias hesternus* (see page 54).

Smilosuchus weren't what you'd call good parents. They would likely abandon their eggs, leaving newly hatched *Smilosuchus* to fend for themselves against other predators, likely by hiding.

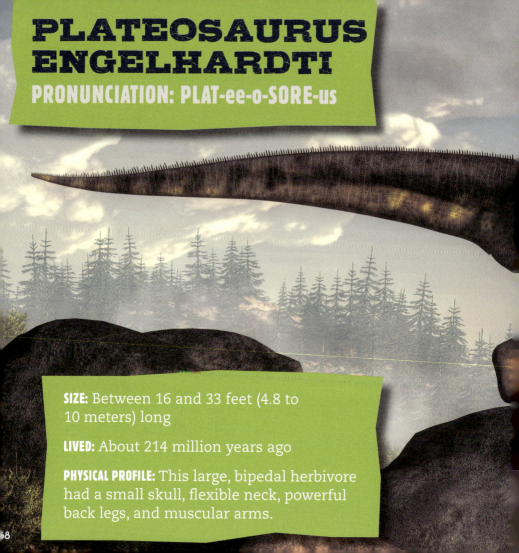

PLATEOSAURUS ENGELHARDTI

PRONUNCIATION: PLAT-ee-o-SORE-us

SIZE: Between 16 and 33 feet (4.8 to 10 meters) long

LIVED: About 214 million years ago

PHYSICAL PROFILE: This large, bipedal herbivore had a small skull, flexible neck, powerful back legs, and muscular arms.

Its bones aren't the only old thing about Plateosaurus. This dinosaur is also one of the oldest known species, with the first mention of it dating as far back as 1837.

BECAUSE SO MANY DIFFERENT REMAINS HAVE BEEN FOUND, PLATEOSAURUS MIGHT HAVE BEEN ONE OF THE MORE COMMON DINOSAURS.

In one dig location in Germany, scientists found nearly complete skeletons of 35 different Plateosaurus, as well as pieces of remains from dozens more.

BUT WHY DOES IT MATTER THAT THERE WERE SO MANY SKELETONS TOGETHER? FINDING LOTS OF DINOSAURS IN ONE PLACE COULD MEAN THAT PLATEOSAURUS LIVED IN HERDS.

This large, heavy dinosaur may have weighed anywhere from 1,300 to 8,800 pounds (590 to 3,992 kilograms).

HAVE YOU HEARD THE PHRASE "STUCK IN THE MUD"? BECAUSE OF ITS HEAVY SIZE, PLATEOSAURUS WOULD HAVE BEEN PRONE TO GETTING STUCK IN ESPECIALLY MUDDY AREAS.

Its thick, leaf-shaped teeth suggest that *Plateosaurus* was an herbivore.

BECAUSE OF ITS POWERFUL HIND LEGS, SCIENTISTS KNOW THIS DINOSAUR LIKELY WALKED ON TWO FEET.

Plateosaurus had sharp claws on its short arms. Although it may have used those claws to hold onto food, they could also have been for defense against predators.

SCIENTISTS CAN TELL THAT MANY OF THE PLATEOSAURUS FOUND LIVED FROM 12 TO 20 YEARS.

Scientists think most *Plateosaurus* were full-grown adults at age 12

PLATEOSAURUS HAD A LONG NECK WITH 10 VERTEBRAE THAT ALLOWED IT TO BE FLEXIBLE, AND THEIR BIG TAIL HAD AT LEAST 40 VERTEBRAE THAT WOULD HAVE ALLOWED IT TO BE MOBILE.

Can you imagine how exhausting it would be walking around on your toes all the time? By looking at the shape of its feet, scientists can tell that *Plateosaurus* walked around on its toes.

THECODONTOSAURUS ANTIQUUS

PRONUNCIATION: THEEK-o-DON-toh-SORE-us

SIZE: About 6 feet (1.8 meters) long

LIVED: Between 227 and 205 million years ago

PHYSICAL PROFILE: This long-tailed herbivore had a large skull and leaf-shaped teeth.

Thecodontosaurus was one of the first dinosaurs discovered. It was noted in 1834.

The first part of this dinosaur's name, *Thecodontosaurus*, means "socket-tooth lizard." The name is a reference to the shape of this dinosaur's teeth.

The second part of its name, *antiquus*, is actually a Latin word that means "ancient." Seems pretty appropriate for a dinosaur!

The first *Thecodontosaurus* fossil, a lower jawbone, was discovered in England.

DON'T GO LOOKING FOR THAT FIRST FOSSIL IN ANY MUSEUM. IT ACTUALLY DOESN'T EXIST ANYMORE. IT WAS DESTROYED DURING THE BOMBINGS OF WORLD WAR II.

Luckily, other fossils of the species survived the war, and more were found in the following years. Scientists have found over 200 different fragments of *Thecodontosaurus* fossils, which has allowed them to reconstruct most of the skeleton of this dinosaur.

ITS LEAF-SHAPED TEETH SUGGEST THAT *THECODONTOSAURUS* MAY HAVE BEEN AN HERBIVORE OR OMNIVORE.

Thecodontosaurus was a bipedal dinosaur, which means it walked on two feet.

THECODONTOSAURUS HAD ARMS THAT WERE MUCH SHORTER THAN ITS LEGS, AND EACH OF ITS HANDS HAD FIVE FINGERS.

THECODONTOSAURUS HAD AN EXCEPTIONALLY LONG TAIL THAT MAY HAVE BEEN LONGER THAN ITS HEAD, NECK, AND BODY PUT TOGETHER.

THIS MIDSIZE DINOSAUR WOULD HAVE WEIGHED ABOUT 24 POUNDS (11 KILOGRAMS).

TRUE OR FALSE

1. T/F **PLACERIAS HESTERNUS WAS ONE OF THE FIERCEST TRIASSIC PREDATORS.**

2. T/F **SMILOSUCHUS GREGORII LOOKED A LOT LIKE A MODERN-DAY CROCODILE.**

3. T/F **PLACERIAS HESTERNUS MIGHT HAVE USED ITS TUSKS TO DEFEND ITSELF FROM AN ATTACKING SMILOSUCHUS.**

4. T/F *PLATEOSAURUS ENGELHARDTI* SOMETIMES GOT STUCK IN MUDDY AREAS BECAUSE OF ITS LARGE SIZE.

5. T/F YOU CAN SEE THE FIRST *THECODONTOSAURUS ANTIQUUS* FOSSIL IN MUSEUMS.

ANSWERS: 1. F; 2. T; 3. T; 4. T; 5. F

JURASSIC PERIOD

201 TO 145 MILLION YEARS AGO

The **JURASSIC PERIOD** marked the start of the age of dinosaurs, and many of the most famous dinos were around during this time. At the end of the Triassic period, another mass extinction wiped out some of the species on Earth, and the supercontinent Pangaea had split into two masses, which were continuing to drift apart throughout the Jurassic period. The changing climate had turned the landscape into lush, humid rainforests, and the shifting land exposed more coastlines. Dinosaurs weren't the only creatures who flourished during this time. More trees meant more prehistoric birds, and more coastlines meant more aquatic creatures. Food sources were diversifying, and competition to be at the top was fierce. During this time period, dinosaurs—now larger and fiercer—started to rule the land.

ALLOSAURUS FRAGILIS

PRONUNCIATION: AL-uh-SAWR-us

Do you have a nickname? During an excavation in Wyoming in 1991, scientists found an *Allosaurus* skeleton that was about 95 percent complete. They nicknamed the dinosaur "Big Al."

SIZE: Up to 30 feet (9 meters) long and 1,000 pounds (454 kilograms)

LIVED: Between 150 and 148 million years ago

PHYSICAL PROFILE: A big predator that grappled prey with strong, three-clawed arms and snapped at flesh with a light, slender skull

Wondering if you've ever seen an *Allosaurus*? In popular culture, *Allosaurus* has appeared in television and movies from *Jurassic World* and *The Land Before Time VI* to *Walking with Dinosaurs* and *Planet Dinosaur*.

SCIENTISTS HAVE FOUND LOTS OF *ALLOSAURUS* FOSSILS, LEADING THEM TO BELIEVE THIS DINOSAUR WAS A COMMON PREDATOR. WHEN FIRST DISCOVERED, IT WAS GIVEN A FEW DIFFERENT NAMES, WHICH LED TO SOME CONFUSION, BUT THE FIRST FOSSIL DESCRIBED WAS FOUND IN COLORADO IN 1869.

In 1996, the same team that found "Big Al" found a second almost complete skeleton. Their nickname this time wasn't the most creative; they called the second dinosaur "Big Al Two."

ALLOSAURUS HAD STRONG ARMS, LARGE HANDS, AND THREE SHARP, HOOKED CLAWS THAT WOULD HAVE ALLOWED IT TO GRAB ONTO PREY.

Its back legs were just as strong, and although it wasn't the fastest of the dinosaurs, scientists think that it would have been faster than many other predators at the time.

WE CAN LEARN A LOT ABOUT DINOSAURS BY LOOKING AT ANIMALS THAT EXIST TODAY. ALLOSAURUS PROBABLY FED LIKE MODERN FALCONS DO, PINNING CARCASSES WITH ITS FEET AND RIPPING OFF CHUNKS OF FLESH WITH POWERFUL JERKS OF ITS NECK.

Allosaurus had short horns over its eyes.

THESE HORNS WEREN'T USED FOR FIGHTING, THOUGH. SCIENTISTS THINK THE HORNS WERE FOR ATTRACTING MATES OR RECOGNIZING OTHER ALLOSAURUS.

Allosaurus had serrated teeth that were about 3 inches (7.6 centimeters) long, which could have easily taken down prey.

ALLOSAURUS WAS HIGH UP ON THE FOOD CHAIN AND WOULD HAVE PREYED ON HERBIVOROUS DINOSAURS AND EVEN SOME OTHER CARNIVORES.

EVEN MIGHTY PREDATORS CAN GET BOO-BOOS! ONE *ALLOSAURUS* TAIL SHOWED SIGNS OF A PARTIALLY HEALED INJURY FROM A *STEGOSAURUS STENOPS* TAIL SPIKE. THIS MAKES IT LIKELY THAT *ALLOSAURUS* HUNTED *STEGOSAURUS*.

At some of the sites where *Allosaurus* remains were discovered, scientists have found fossils from more than one *Allosaurus*.

THIS GROUPING COULD MEAN THAT *ALLOSAURUS* WOULD HUNT IN PACKS TO GANG UP ON PREY.

Another interpretation of this discovery is less friendly. Some scientists think *Allosaurus* may have become aggressive toward other *Allosaurus* when they were fighting over the same prey.

DURING THE JURASSIC PERIOD, *ALLOSAURUS* MAY HAVE BEEN VERY COMMON— AND FEARSOME—CARNIVORES. FOSSILS HAVE BEEN DISCOVERED IN VARIOUS LOCATIONS IN NORTH AMERICA.

Along with *Tyrannosaurus rex* (see page 230), *Allosaurus* is considered to be one of the most well-known carnivorous dinosaurs, and *Allosaurus* skeletons can be found in many museums.

IN UTAH *ALLOSAURUS* IS EVEN THE OFFICIAL STATE FOSSIL.

If you ever take a trip to Utah, you could see a fossil *Allosaurus*. The Natural History Museum in Utah has multiple *Allosaurus* specimens ranging in age from baby to adult.

BY STUDYING SKELETONS OF DIFFERENT AGES, SCIENTISTS CAN BETTER UNDERSTAND HOW *ALLOSAURUS* GREW THROUGHOUT ITS LIFE.

Based on those studies, scientists think *Allosaurus* may have been full grown at about 15 years old and would have lived to be somewhere between 22 to 28 years old.

DILOPHOSAURUS WETHERILLI

PRONUNCIATION: DY-low-pho-SAWR-us

In Rocky Hill, Connecticut, at Dinosaur State Park you can find a life-size reconstruction of *Dilophosaurus*. In 2017, Connecticut named *Dilophosaurus* their official state dinosaur.

FOSSILS FROM A SECOND SPECIES OF *DILOPHOSAURUS*, *DILOPHOSAURUS SINENSIS*, HAVE BEEN DISCOVERED IN CHINA.

SIZE: About 23 feet (7 meters) long and 1,000 pounds (454 kilograms)

LIVED: About 193 million years ago

PHYSICAL PROFILE: A slender, medium-sized predator immediately recognizable by the thin, paired crests on top of its head

POP CULTURE REFERENCES HAVE LED TO THIS DINOSAUR BEING VERY MISUNDERSTOOD. *DILOPHOSAURUS* DIDN'T HAVE A NECK FRILL OR SPIT VENOM LIKE IN *JURASSIC PARK*.

> In reality, *Dilophosaurus* had a pretty weak bite. Its jaw wasn't very powerful, although its back teeth were sharp for slicing. It likely could have killed smaller prey, but taking down larger prey would have required it to use its hands and feet.

MOST OF WHAT WE KNOW ABOUT *DILOPHOSAURUS* COMES FROM THE DINOSAUR'S BONES. BUT THERE'S ANOTHER KIND OF EVIDENCE PALEONTOLOGISTS CAN STUDY TO LEARN ABOUT DINOSAUR LIVES: TRACE FOSSILS. THESE ARE TRACKS AND OTHER TRACES THAT REFLECT PREHISTORIC BEHAVIOR.

At one site in southern Utah, paleontologists have uncovered a spot where a *Dilophosaurus*—or very similar dinosaur—laid down for a rest. The rock shows marks from the dinosaur's tail, hip, feet, and hands as it sat by the side of a lake, eventually shuffling forward and walking off along the shore. This trace is the closest we can get to watching a living *Dilophosaurus*.

DILOPHOSAURUS HAD POWERFUL ARMS THAT WOULD HAVE BEEN HELPFUL IN GRABBING PREY. ITS HANDS HAD FOUR FINGERS, BUT THE FOURTH FINGER WASN'T FUNCTIONAL.

Dilophosaurus may have even been a scavenger dinosaur, feeding on animals it found already dead.

COMPARED TO OTHER DINOSAURS AT THE TIME, DILOPHOSAURUS WAS A MIDSIZE DINOSAUR. THE MODERN BROWN BEAR IS ABOUT THE SAME SIZE.

The first fossils of *Dilophosaurus* showed up in 1940 in Arizona. Over the next few years, scientists discovered more *Dilophosaurus* fossils, including one almost complete skeleton.

THE NAME "*DILOPHOSAURUS*" MEANS "TWO-CRESTED LIZARD."

It's pretty obvious why it was named that: *Dilophosaurus* had two crests on its head over its eyes.

SCIENTISTS AREN'T SURE WHY EXACTLY *DILOPHOSAURUS* HAD THESE CRESTS. THEY WOULDN'T HAVE BEEN USEFUL IN A BATTLE, BUT THEY MAY HAVE BEEN USED IN CHOOSING A MATE OR IDENTIFYING OTHER *DILOPHOSAURUS*.

ANOTHER THEORY SUGGESTS THAT THE CRESTS MAY HAVE BEEN USEFUL IN HELPING TO REGULATE TEMPERATURE, ALTHOUGH SCIENTISTS THINK THAT'S NOT AS LIKELY.

IF YOU'VE EVER LOST A BABY TOOTH, YOU HAVE SOMETHING IN COMMON WITH *DILOPHOSAURUS*! THIS DINOSAUR WOULD LOSE ITS TEETH AND REPLACE THEM WITH NEW, HEALTHIER TEETH.

GUANLONG WUCAII

PRONUNCIATION: GWAN-long

By studying an adult skeleton, scientists determined that *Guanlong* was fully grown at about seven years old.

SIZE: Almost 10 feet (3 meters) long

LIVED: About 160 million years ago

PHYSICAL PROFILE: A small tyrannosaur with long arms, a shallow skull, and a prominent crest jutting from its face

WHAT DO YOU THINK OF WHEN YOU HEAR "TYRANNOSAUR"? WE OFTEN THINK OF TYRANNOSAURS AS GIANT CARNIVORES WITH HUGE HEADS AND TINY ARMS. BACK IN THE JURASSIC PERIOD, HOWEVER, TYRANNOSAURS WERE SMALL PREDATORS WITH VERY DIFFERENT PROPORTIONS. ONE OF THE EARLIEST WAS *GUANLONG*—A TYRANT DINOSAUR WITH LONG ARMS, A SHALLOW SNOUT, A PROMINENT CREST ON ITS HEAD, AND A COAT OF DINOFUZZ ON ITS BODY.

Unlike later tyrannosaurs, *Guanlong* had long arms with three fingers that would have been useful for ripping and grabbing.

Guanlong lived about 90 million years before the most famous of the tyrannosaurs, *Tyrannosaurus rex* (see page 230).

THE FIRST *GUANLONG* WAS DISCOVERED IN A DESERT IN CHINA IN 2002.

Talk about a tough way to go. The first *Guanlong* skeletons were found in a weird death trap—a huge mud hole made by the footprint of a long-necked sauropod.

THESE SKELETONS WERE ACTUALLY DIFFERENT AGES, AND BOTH WERE ALMOST COMPLETE.

One skeleton was of a young *Guanlong* about 6 years old, and the other was an adult about 12 years old.

THE YOUNG *GUANLONG* HAD A MUCH SHORTER CREST COMPARED TO THE MORE EXTENSIVE CREST ON THE ADULT *GUANLONG*.

Guanlong and its early tyrannosaur relatives elsewhere lived in environments dominated by the much bigger *Allosaurus fragilis* (see page 70) and other predators, and it was only much later, during the Cretaceous period, that tyrannosaurs got large enough to rule.

THEY MAY NOT HAVE BEEN KING OF THE LAND, BUT *GUANLONG* DID HAVE A CROWN. THE NAME *GUANLONG* COMES FROM THE CHINESE WORDS FOR "CROWNED DRAGON."

Along its snout, *Guanlong* has a long, crown-like crest that was likely just for show rather than function.

ITS CREST WAS THIN AND DELICATE, MAKING IT UNLIKELY THAT THEY COULD HAVE BEEN FUNCTIONAL. THEY WERE MADE UP OF NASAL BONES AND AIR SACS, AND THEY HAVE SIMILAR CHARACTERISTICS TO TRAITS ON MODERN BIRDS.

Another trait that tied *Guanlong* to birds is that it likely had feathers.

GUANLONG WAS UNDOUBTEDLY A PREDATOR, BUT IT LIKELY WASN'T AS FEROCIOUS AS OTHER HUNTERS OF THE TIME.

If you had to choose between speed and strength, which would you pick? One skill that would have benefitted *Guanlong* was its speed, which would have allowed it to outrun enemies with ease.

CRYOLOPHOSAURUS ELLIOTI

PRONUNCIATION: CRY-uh-LOW-pho-SAWR-us

SIZE: About 21 feet (6.4 meters) long and 1,000 pounds (454 kilograms)

LIVED: About 190 million years ago

PHYSICAL PROFILE: A midsize carnivore with a deep skull, three-clawed hands, and a ridged crest atop its head

Like other crested dinosaurs, the crest of *Cryolophosaurus* was very fragile, which meant it was likely just used in mating displays or to identify other *Cryolophosaurus*.

Have you ever seen a picture of Elvis? If you have, try to imagine his signature hairdo, and you'll be able to picture this dinosaur. The paleontologists who discovered *Cryolophosaurus* were so impressed with its bony pompadour that they nicknamed the animal "Elvisaurus."

THE BONES OF *CRYOLOPHOSAURUS* WERE FOUND IN WHAT MIGHT SEEM LIKE A VERY UNUSUAL PLACE FOR A DINOSAUR: ANTARCTICA.

The discovery in 1991 marked the first dinosaur from that continent to be formally named.

IMAGINE LIVING IN ANTARCTICA! TODAY, THE COLD, ROCKY HABITAT WHERE THE FOSSILS WERE FOUND IS UNLIVABLE, BUT DURING THE JURASSIC PERIOD THE SAME LAND WAS MUCH CLOSER TO THE EQUATOR, AND JURASSIC ANTARCTICA EVEN HAD LUSH FORESTS WHERE *CRYOLOPHOSAURUS* AND BIG, LONG-NECKED SAUROPOD DINOSAURS SUCH AS *GLACIALISAURUS HAMMERI* ROAMED.

UNSURPRISINGLY, THE NAME *CRYOLOPHOSAURUS* MEANS "COLD CRESTED LIZARD." THE "COLD" IS A REFERENCE TO ITS PREFERRED HABITAT, AND THE "CRESTED" REFERS TO THE HAIRLIKE CREST ON ITS HEAD.

The crest had a somewhat comblike appearance and is actually made from an extension of its skull bones fused onto horns coming up near its eye sockets.

COMPARED TO OTHER DINOSAURS WITH CRESTS, THE CREST PLACEMENT ON *CRYOLOPHOSAURUS* IS UNUSUAL. OTHERS TYPICALLY RUN ALONG THE SKULL RATHER THAN STRAIGHT ACROSS.

Eating too quickly is always dangerous—even for dinosaurs! One *Cryolophosaurus* was found with what appeared to be a rib from its prey lodged in its throat, leading scientists to believe it may have choked to death.

DESPITE ITS LARGE SIZE, SCANS OF A *CRYOLOPHOSAURUS* SKULL SHOW THAT IT LIKELY HAD A VERY SMALL BRAIN IN COMPARISON.

ANCHIORNIS HUXLEYI
PRONUNCIATION: ANK-ee-OR-niss

SIZE: A foot (0.3 meters) long, about the size of a common crow

LIVED: About 160 million years ago

PHYSICAL PROFILE: With long arms, a little sickle claw on each foot, and tiny teeth, the feathery *Anchiornis* fluttered after insects and other small prey.

HAVE YOU EVER TRIED TO CLIMB A TREE? IT'S NOT AS EASY AS IT LOOKS! ALTHOUGH IT WASN'T VERY FAST, *ANCHIORNIS* HAD CLAWED FEET THAT WOULD HAVE BEEN HELPFUL FOR CLIMBING TREES.

The first *Anchiornis* fossils were found in China in 2009.

The name *Anchiornis* means "near bird," and is likely a reference to the fact that this creature is one of the nearest prehistoric relatives to birds.

IN FACT, SCIENTISTS THINK THAT *ANCHIORNIS* CAN ANSWER A LOT OF QUESTIONS ABOUT HOW BIRDS TRANSITIONED TO BEING ABLE TO FLY.

Anchiornis wouldn't have won many races. You might think Anchiornis would be a fast runner with its long legs, but having a lot of feathers on its legs would have slowed it down.

DURING THE JURASSIC PERIOD, DINOSAURS WERE GETTING FLUFFY AND FUZZY. DINOFUZZ— THE WISPY PRECURSOR TO TRUE FEATHERS— WAS A COMMON FEATURE OF CARNIVOROUS DINOSAURS.

This prehistoric fluff helped keep dinosaurs warm and was also useful in display.

BUT, BECAUSE THE FEATHERS ON *ANCHIORNIS* WERE SO SMALL AND SHORT, IT WOULDN'T HAVE BEEN ABLE TO FLY LONG DISTANCES.

ALTHOUGH IT COULDN'T REALLY FLY FOR LONG DISTANCES LIKE MODERN BIRDS, *ANCHIORNIS* COULD FLUTTER AND GLIDE.

Have you been wondering how dinosaurs are related to birds? *Anchiornis* is one of the dinosaurs that proves it! Thanks to beautifully preserved dinosaurs like *Anchiornis*, paleontologists know that birds—including every bird alive today—are really predatory dinosaurs. The first birds evolved about 150 million years ago, late in the Jurassic period, and lived alongside the rest of their dinosaurian family until another extinction at the end of the Cretaceous period wiped out all the non-bird dinosaurs.

WE DON'T KNOW WHAT COLORS MOST DINOSAURS REALLY WERE. *ANCHIORNIS* IS AN EXCEPTION. PALEONTOLOGISTS HAVE BEEN ABLE TO WORK OUT THIS LITTLE DINOSAUR'S COLORS THANKS TO ITS FEATHERS.

Just like modern birds, *Anchiornis* had colors created by tiny structures on its feathers called melanosomes.

BECAUSE THESE STRUCTURES MAKE COLORS, PALEONTOLOGISTS HAVE BEEN ABLE TO COMPARE THE FEATHERS OF *ANCHIORNIS* WITH THOSE OF MODERN BIRDS.

Scientists found that *Anchiornis* was mostly black with white patches on its wings and a splash of red on its head. This made it look like a punk rock magpie, complete with teeth and claws.

STEGOSAURUS STENOPS
PRONUNCIATION: STEG-oh-SORE-us

SIZE: About 30 feet (9 meters) long

LIVED: About 155 to 150 million years ago

PHYSICAL PROFILE: This large herbivore had an iconic row of leaf-shaped bony plates along its back and a spiked tail.

EVEN SCIENTISTS MAKE MISTAKES! WHEN *STEGOSAURUS* WAS ORIGINALLY DISCOVERED, SCIENTISTS MISTAKENLY THOUGHT ITS BONY PLATES LAID FLAT ALONG ITS BACK. THEY CALLED IT THE "ROOFED LIZARD" BECAUSE THEY THOUGHT THE PLATES WERE LIKE THE SHINGLES ON A ROOF.

Stegosaurus was part of a group of dinosaurs called *Thyreophora* that were known for having body armor, which also includes *Ankylosaurus magniventris* (see page 234).

After finding a *Stegosaurus* skeleton that had been preserved in mud with the plates in their proper, upright position, scientists realized that their first descriptions of this creature were incorrect.

STEGOSAURUS PLATES WERE MADE FROM A BONY MATERIAL THAT WASN'T ENTIRELY SOLID, CALLED OSTEODERMS. THERE WOULD LIKELY HAVE BEEN BLOOD VESSELS RUNNING ALONG THE PLATES.

When you think about a *Stegosaurus*, you might imagine tons and tons of those pointed plates along their backs, but they didn't really have that many! Each *Stegosaurus* only had 17 plates in two rows along its back with a pointed part facing upward.

STEGOSAURUS PLATES ARE SOMETIMES CALLED SCUTES, AND SCIENTISTS DEBATE WHAT THEY WERE REALLY FOR. ALTHOUGH ONE THEORY SAYS THAT THE POINTED TIPS MADE THEM USEFUL FOR PROTECTION, ANOTHER SAYS THAT THE BLOOD VESSELS IN THE PLATES COULD BE A SIGN THAT THEY WERE USED FOR TEMPERATURE REGULATION. ANOTHER THEORY SAYS THEY WERE JUST THERE FOR A MATING DISPLAY.

What do you think *Stegosaurus* used its plates for? There is some weight to the theory that they were for defense. With predators like *Allosaurus fragilis* (see page 68) around attacking *Stegosaurus*, it would have needed to be strong to survive an attack.

STEGOSAURUS WAS LARGE AND SLOW MOVING, BUT IT KNEW HOW TO DEFEND ITSELF FROM PREDATORS. ITS SPIKED TAIL WAS A GOOD DEFENSE AGAINST ATTACKING PREDATORS.

Scientists have a lot of evidence to study to learn about *Stegosaurus*. Fossils from 80 different *Stegosaurus* have been found in the United States and Portugal.

COMPARED TO THE SIZE OF ITS BODY, STEGOSAURUS HAD A RELATIVELY SMALL BRAIN. IN FACT, IT MAY HAVE HAD ONE OF THE LOWEST BRAIN-TO-BODY RATIOS OF ALL DINOSAURS.

Can you picture a *Stegosaurus*? Because we can really understand what *Stegosaurus* looked like thanks to a well-preserved skeleton, it's one of the most common dinosaurs to appear in popular culture, including in the movie *King Kong*.

TRUE OR FALSE

1. T / F SCIENTISTS HAVE DISCOVERED AN ALMOST COMPLETE *ALLOSAURUS FRAGILIS* SKELETON THAT THEY NICKNAMED "BIG AL."

2. T / F *DILOPHOSAURUS WETHERILLI* WAS A VENOMOUS DINOSAUR.

3. T / F *CRYOLOPHOSAURUS ELLIOTI* HAS ALSO BEEN CALLED "ELVISAURUS" BECAUSE IT HAS A FACIAL CREST THAT LOOKS LIKE A HAIRDO.

4. T/F ANCHIORNIS HUXLEYI IS A PREHISTORIC RELATIVE OF MODERN BIRDS.

5. T/F STEGOSAURUS STENOPS HAD HUNDREDS OF POINTED PLATES ALONG ITS BACK.

ANSWERS: 1. T, 2. F, 3. F, 4. T, 5. F

APATOSAURUS AJAX

PRONUNCIATION: uh-PAT-uh-SORE-us

SIZE: About 60 to 75 feet (18 to 22.8 meters) long

LIVED: About 152 million years ago

PHYSICAL PROFILE: This herbivore was a standard sauropod with a bulky body, long neck, and long tail.

Based on its habitat, *Apatosaurus* likely ate ferns, plants, and even algae.

Apatosaurus is easily confused with another member of the sauropod family, *Brontosaurus excelsus* (see page 98), but the two are considered different species by some scientists, though there is still debate about how different they really are.

This herbivorous dinosaur was a member of the sauropod family.

APATOSAURUS, WHICH MEANS "DECEPTIVE LIZARD," WAS FIRST NAMED IN 1877 AFTER A NEARLY COMPLETE SKELETON WAS DISCOVERED.

Have you ever heard the phrase "looks can be deceiving"? The name *Apatosaurus* came from the fact that it had unusually shaped bones. Those bones made *Apatosaurus* look like an aquatic animal, but scientists quickly realized that they shouldn't be deceived—*Apatosaurus* was definitely a dinosaur.

Apatosaurus fossils have been found all around the United States, including in Colorado, Oklahoma, New Mexico, Wyoming, and Utah.

Their bones weren't the only thing about *Apatosaurus* that made scientists think they were water-dwellers. Based on where the fossils were found, *Apatosaurus* likely lived near riverbanks. Scientists once thought that they may have been able to swim or live in the water, but newer research shows that they probably stayed on land.

ALTHOUGH THEIR NECKS APPEAR TO BE MOBILE, ONE OF THE BIGGEST DEBATES ABOUT *APATOSAURUS* AND OTHER SAUROPODS COMES FROM HOW FLEXIBLE THEIR NECKS WERE. ALTHOUGH IT WAS ONCE THOUGHT THAT THEIR NECKS WERE STIFF, COMPARISONS TO MODERN ANIMALS LIKE SWANS SHOWS THAT THEY MAY HAVE HAD FLEXIBLE "S"-SHAPED NECKS.

BRONTOSAURUS EXCELSUS

PRONUNCIATION: BRAWN-toe-SORE-us

SIZE: Up to 72 feet (22 meters) long

LIVED: About 152 million years ago

PHYSICAL PROFILE: A heavy long-necked, long-tailed herbivorous sauropod

As of 2015, some scientists declared that *Brontosaurus* was different enough from *Apatosaurus ajax* (see page 96) to be considered its own species, but plenty of scientists debate this fact!

Look out, it's a headless dinosaur! Scientists haven't yet discovered a *Brontosaurus* skull, but they can guess what it would have looked like by comparing *Brontosaurus* to relatives like *Apatosaurus*.

HAVE YOU EVER BEEN MISTAKEN FOR SOMEONE ELSE? SCIENTISTS HAVE LONG DEBATED WHETHER *BRONTOSAURUS* AND *APATOSAURUS* SHOULD BE CONSIDERED THE SAME SPECIES. BOTH SAUROPODS AND HAVE SIMILAR TRAITS, SO IT'S EASY TO SEE WHY THEY WOULD BE CONFUSED FOR ONE ANOTHER.

There are actually three different species of *Brontosaurus*, which vary in size.

Brontosaurus fossils have been found throughout North America, especially in what's known as the Morrison Basin, which stretches from New Mexico to Alberta, Canada.

As is typical of the sauropod family, *Brontosaurus* had a heavy body, pillar-like feet used to walk on all fours, and a very long neck.

DIPLODOCUS CARNEGII
PRONUNCIATION: DIP-low-DOCK-us

SIZE: Up to 85 feet (26 meters) long

LIVED: About 152 million years ago

PHYSICAL PROFILE: A typical sauropod, *Diplodocus* has a long neck and long tail as well as a bulky body on four, pillar-like legs.

Diplodocus would have lived alongside its relatives, the *Apatosaurus ajax* (see page 96) and *Brontosaurus excelsus* (see page 98).

These herbivores would have used their long necks to grab leaves and plants.

Sauropods like *Diplodocus* have an incredibly identifiable body type with long necks and long tails.

DIPLODOCUS FOSSILS HAVE BEEN FOUND IN NORTH AMERICA ALONG WHAT'S KNOWN AS THE MORRISON FORMATION.

The name *Diplodocus* actually means "double-beamed" and refers to its chevron-shaped bones.

IN POP CULTURE, THERE'S A FAMOUS DJ KNOWN AS DIPLO. THE NAME IS A SHORTENED FORM OF *DIPLODOCUS*, AND HE PICKED IT BECAUSE OF HIS CHILDHOOD LOVE FOR THIS DINOSAUR!

There are three species of *Diplodocus*, but the most well known is *Diplodocus carnegii*, which was named after philanthropist Andrew Carnegie. Carnegie donated plaster casts to museums, which allowed this species to be put on display.

ONE FAMOUS CAST, FONDLY KNOWN AS DIPPY, HAS HELPED TO MAKE THIS DINOSAUR FAMOUS IN MUSEUMS.

Although Dippy is usually on display at the Carnegie Museum of Natural History in Pittsburgh, it is on display on a "tour" of various cities in the United Kingdon from 2018 to 2020.

WHEN DIPPY WAS FIRST DISPLAYED, ITS TAIL WAS DOWN LOW TO THE GROUND. BUT AS SCIENTISTS LEARNED THAT THE TAIL WAS LIKELY RAISED FOR BALANCE, MUSEUM CURATORS REALIZED THEY WOULD NEED TO ADJUST THE CAST ON DISPLAY. BY 1993 THE TAIL WAS RAISED TO ACCURATELY REFLECT ITS POSITION BALANCING OUT THE NECK.

Although once separate species, the dinosaur commonly known as *Seismosaurus hallorum* was declared to actually be a species of *Diplodocus* in 2004. It's now known as *Diplodocus hallorum*.

CAMARASAURUS SUPREMUS

PRONUNCIATION: KAM-or-o-SAWR-os

SIZE: Up to 75 feet (22.8 meters) long

LIVED: Between 155 and 145 million years ago

PHYSICAL PROFILE: *Camarasaurus* has a large body, long tail, and long neck like other sauropods. It also has a blunt snout and arched head that makes its skull look square.

First discovered in 1877, it was named *Camarasaurus*, meaning "chambered lizard."

SCIENTISTS WERE LUCKY ENOUGH TO FIND FOSSILS THAT SHOWED THEM THE SHAPE OF A *CAMARASAURUS* SKULL, WHICH WAS CERTAINLY A RARE FIND. THEY WERE ABLE TO DETERMINE THAT *CAMARASAURUS* HAD A BLUNT SNOUT AND ARCHED SKULL, WHICH MAKES ITS HEAD LOOK SQUARE.

LIKE OTHER SAUROPODS, *CAMARASAURUS* HAD FRONT LEGS THAT WERE SHORTER THAN ITS HIND LEGS, BUT *CAMARASAURUS* ALSO HAD AN INTERESTING BODY SHAPE WHERE ITS SHOULDER BLADES WERE LOW AND ITS HIPS WERE HIGH. THIS WOULD HAVE ALLOWED ITS LEGS TO SOMEWHAT LINE UP EVEN THOUGH THEY WEREN'T THE SAME LENGTH.

Like other sauropods, *Camarasaurus* may have traveled around in small herds for safety from predators.

This sauropod is one of the most common, and its fossils from North America are well preserved.

THOUGH IT WAS BIG, *CAMARASAURUS* WASN'T SAFE FROM PREDATORS. *ALLOSAURUS FRAGILIS* (SEE PAGE 70) LIKELY HUNTED DOWN THIS DINOSAUR, AND ONE FOSSIL OF A *CAMARASAURUS* PELVIS FOUND IN UTAH EVEN HAD MARKS THAT CAME FROM *ALLOSAURUS* TEETH!

Who's the tallest of your family? Compared to other dinosaurs, *Camarasaurus* is large, but compared to other sauropods like *Diplodocus carnegii* (see page 100), it's definitely not the largest of the sauropod family.

WHEN YOU LOOK AT THEIR LONG NECKS, YOU MIGHT WONDER HOW SAUROPODS HELD UP THEIR HEADS. THOSE LONG SAUROPOD NECKS HAVE A UNIQUE STRUCTURE WITH HOLLOW CHAMBERS BETWEEN THE VERTEBRAE, HELPING THE BONES IN THEIR NECK TO BE BOTH STRONG AND LIGHT.

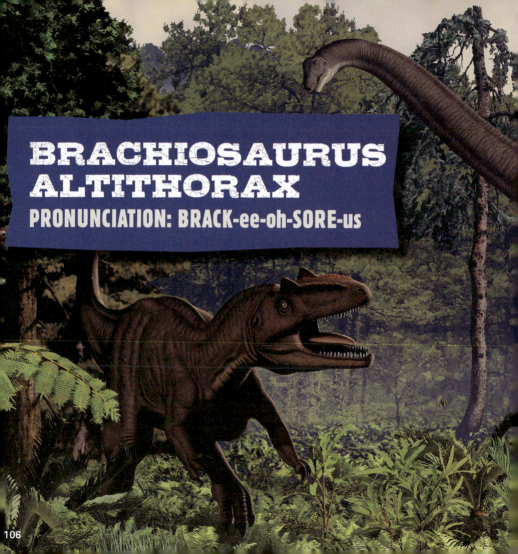

BRACHIOSAURUS ALTITHORAX

PRONUNCIATION: BRACK-ee-oh-SORE-us

SIZE: About 59 to 69 feet (18 to 21 meters) long

LIVED: About 154 million years ago

PHYSICAL PROFILE: A sauropod with a long neck and tail, *Brachiosaurus* had front legs that were longer than its back legs.

Brachiosaurus was first described in 1903 after fossils were discovered in Colorado. Since then, more fossils have been uncovered throughout the United States.

LIKE OTHER SAUROPOD DINOSAURS, BRACHIOSAURUS WOULD HAVE WALKED ON ALL FOURS AND HAD A LARGE BODY AND A LONG NECK AND TAIL.

One key difference between *Brachiosaurus* and other sauropod dinosaurs is that, although other sauropod species had front legs that were shorter than the back, which caused them to lean slightly forward, *Brachiosaurus* had front legs that were longer than its hind legs. This actually meant that *Brachiosaurus* would be tipped slightly upward when standing.

HAVE YOU EVER PICTURED A LIZARD WITH ARMS? ITS LONG FRONT LEGS GAVE *BRACHIOSAURUS* ITS NAME, WHICH MEANS "ARM LIZARD."

Even if you stand on your tiptoes, you can probably only reach things a little bit off the ground. Thanks to its long neck and tall legs, *Brachiosaurus* may have been able to eat vegetation as high as 30 feet (9 meters) off the ground!

BRACHIOSAURUS HAD A WIDE, THICK JAW FILLED WITH SPOON-LIKE TEETH THAT WOULD HAVE BEEN USEFUL FOR STRIPPING LEAVES OFF BRANCHES.

Brachiosaurus was an incredibly heavy dinosaur that would have weighed tens of thousands of pounds (or kilograms)!

THAT MUCH EATING COULD QUICKLY STRIP THE TREES BARE. SCIENTISTS THINK *BRACHIOSAURUS* MAY HAVE TRAVELED IN HERDS, MOVING TO A NEW PLACE ONCE THE OLD ONE RAN OUT OF VEGETATION.

Have you ever gotten full after eating a really big meal? To keep up its weight, *Brachiosaurus* and other sauropods may have eaten as much as 880 pounds (400 kilograms) of vegetation a day!

BRACHIOSAURUS WAS ONCE THOUGHT TO BE ONE OF THE LARGEST DINOSAURS, AND ALTHOUGH LARGER SPECIES HAVE SINCE EMERGED, IT'S STILL WELL KNOWN FOR ITS SIZE.

On the screen, *Brachiosaurus* made a notable appearance in the movie *Jurassic Park*.

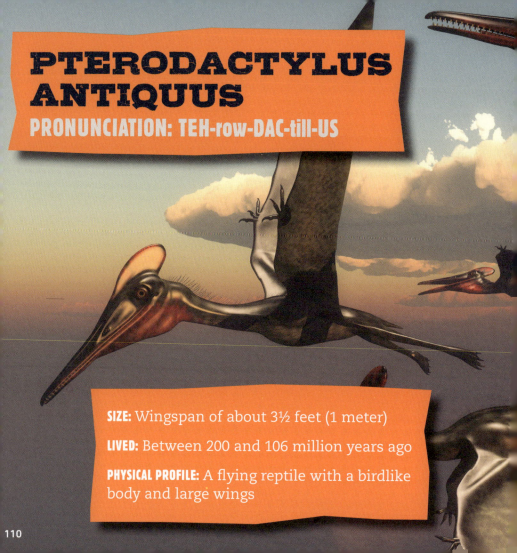

PTERODACTYLUS ANTIQUUS

PRONUNCIATION: TEH-row-DAC-till-US

SIZE: Wingspan of about 3½ feet (1 meter)

LIVED: Between 200 and 106 million years ago

PHYSICAL PROFILE: A flying reptile with a birdlike body and large wings

Have you ever heard of a pterodactyl? It's actually not one specific dinosaur! Pterodactyl is the common name for a group of winged reptiles call pterosaurs, and there are about 130 different members in this family. *Pterodactylus antiquus* was one of the vicious flying reptiles that roamed the air.

DOES THIS CREATURE REMIND YOU OF A BIRD? ALTHOUGH IT MIGHT LOOK LIKE A MODERN BIRD, *PTERODACTYLUS* WASN'T REALLY RELATED TO BIRDS. IN FACT, MODERN BIRDS DESCENDED FROM SMALL, FEATHERED, LAND-BASED DINOSAURS, NOT FROM FLYING REPTILES LIKE *PTERODACTYLUS*.

When it was first discovered in 1784, scientists thought *Pterodactylus* may have used its wings as paddles and lived in the water.

BY 1801, SCIENTISTS HAD REALIZED THAT *PTERODACTYLUS* COULD, IN FACT, FLY.

Of the specimens found, scientists think that they may not yet have uncovered a fully grown adult.

THE NAME *PTERODACTYLUS* MEANS "WINGED FINGER," AND THIS DESCRIPTION IS VERY ACCURATE TO HOW THE WINGS STRETCH OVER THIS CREATURE'S ELONGATED FINGERS.

Pterodactylus likely had a long neck that would have been useful for catching prey, and this reptile was undoubtedly a carnivore that ate small animals.

PTERODACTYLUS HAD A LONG BEAK AS WELL AS TEETH.

DINO QUIZ

1. WHICH TWO SPECIES WERE ONCE CONSIDERED TO BE THE SAME DINOSAUR?

A. APATOSAURUS AJAX AND BRACHIOSAURUS ALTITHORAX

B. APATOSAURUS AJAX AND BRONTOSAURUS EXCELSUS

C. BRACHIOSAURUS ALTITHORAX AND CAMARASAURUS SUPREMUS

D. DIPLODOCUS CARNEGII AND BRONTOSAURUS EXCELSUS

2. WHICH DINOSAUR HAS A FAMOUS CAST KNOWN AS DIPPY?

A. DILOPHOSAURUS WETHERILLI

B. APATOSAURUS AJAX

C. DIPLODOCUS CARNEGII

D. PTERODACTYLUS ANTIQUUS

3. WHICH OF THE FOLLOWING IS NOT A MEMBER OF THE SAUROPOD FAMILY?

A. *DIPLODOCUS CARNEGII*

B. *APATOSAURUS AJAX*

C. *PTERODACTYLUS ANTIQUUS*

D. *CAMARASAURUS SUPREMUS*

4. HOW BIG COULD *DIPLODOCUS CARNEGII* GROW TO BE?

A. 85 FEET (26 METERS)

B. 75 FEET (23 METERS)

C. 65 FEET (20 METERS)

D. 55 FEET (16¾ METERS)

5. WHAT TYPE OF ANIMAL DOES *PTERODACTYLUS ANTIQUUS* LOOK LIKE (EVEN THOUGH THEY AREN'T RELATED)?

A. WHALES

B. CROCODILES

C. SHARKS

D. BIRDS

Answers: 1. B; 2. C; 3. C; 4. A; 5. D

CRETACEOUS PERIOD

145 TO 66 MILLION YEARS AGO

By the Cretaceous period, dinosaurs were the ruling class, and this was their time to thrive. The climate was gradually warming, and sea levels were rising as continents continued to drift farther apart, which led to more abundant plants and food sources. Animal species, especially dinosaurs, were more diverse than ever, and insects were starting to appear on the landscape. But all good things come to an end, and the era of dinosaurs was no exception. At the end of the Cretaceous period, a mass extinction wiped out nearly 75 percent of the existing species, including any nonflying dinosaurs. But the ones that did survive eventually evolved into modern birds! By studying chemicals in Earth's crust, scientists know that an asteroid struck Earth at about the same time that the mass extinction took place. That kind of an impact could have suddenly turned the climate cold and unlivable, which could explain why so many species disappeared at the same time.

VELOCIRAPTOR MONGOLIENSIS
PRONUNCIATION: VEL-oss-EE-RAP-tor

SIZE: Turkey-sized, or about 7 feet (2 meters) long from nose to tail

LIVED: Between 75 and 71 million years ago

PHYSICAL PROFILE: An iconic raptor with grasping hands, stiff tail, and an extendable toe tipped with a large claw on the inside of each foot

This reptile's feathers would have been for display, or possibly even for warmth.

EVEN AMONG THE DINOSAURS, VELOCIRAPTOR IS A SUPERSTAR! THIS DINOSAUR WAS MADE FAMOUS BY THE MOVIE JURASSIC PARK, BUT IT WAS FIRST DISCOVERED IN 1922 IN MONGOLIA.

Are you picturing a giant dinosaur? Although you might think it is much larger based on *Jurassic Park*, *Velociraptor* was actually only about the size of a turkey.

ANOTHER MOVIE MISTAKE IS THAT THE *VELOCIRAPTOR* YOU SEE ON-SCREEN DOESN'T HAVE ANY FEATHERS, BUT SCIENTISTS THINK THIS DINOSAUR LIKELY HAD SOME BIRDLIKE PLUMAGE.

Velociraptor laid its eggs in nests, and its feathers may have allowed it to keep the nest warm before the eggs hatched.

SO, IF *VELOCIRAPTOR* HAD FEATHERS, COULD IT FLY? EVEN WITH FEATHERS, *VELOCIRAPTOR* WOULDN'T HAVE BEEN ABLE TO FLY. IT HAD ARMS, NOT WINGS.

While *Velociraptor* walked, its long claws would have pointed upright. Then, when it attacked, its claws would snap downward.

***VELOCIRAPTOR* MAY HAVE ATTACKED SIMILARLY TO MODERN BIRDS OF PREY. IT COULD HAVE LEAPED ONTO AND USED ITS BODY WEIGHT TO WEIGH DOWN ITS PREY, AND THEN GRIPPED ON USING ITS CLAWS.**

ONE INTERESTING FOSSIL DISCOVERY REVEALED A *VELOCIRAPTOR* AND A *PROTOCERATOPS ANDREWSI* TRAPPED FOREVER MID-FIGHT. SCIENTISTS THINK THEY MAY HAVE BEEN CAUGHT IN A SANDSTORM AND SUDDENLY KILLED, PRESERVING THEM AS THEY WERE.

Velociraptor would have hunted all sorts of animals and lizards, both large and small.

The name *Velociraptor* means "swift robber," because these dinosaurs were very fast, carnivorous hunters.

Bumps along fossilized *Velociraptor* forearms show where feathers would have been anchored.

This reptile's long tail was somewhat stiff and was probably also used for balancing.

VELOCIRAPTOR DIDN'T ONLY HUNT. DAMAGED BONES FOUND IN FOSSILS SHOW THAT THIS DINOSAUR WOULD SCAVENGE WHEN IT HAD THE CHANCE.

The long claw *Velociraptor* has on each foot would have been used to tackle and trap its prey.

WHILE ON TOP OF ITS PREY, IT MAY HAVE FLAPPED ITS FEATHERED ARMS TO HELP BALANCE.

Though it had incredibly strong arms and sharp claws, *Velociraptor* also had a mouth full of teeth that would have been effective weapons.

MOST LIKELY, *VELOCIRAPTOR* WOULDN'T HAVE USED THOSE TEETH FOR CHEWING. INSTEAD, IT LIKELY TORE OFF AND SWALLOWED LARGE GULPS OF FOOD.

Like modern birds, *Velociraptor* was probably somewhat warm-blooded.

VELOCIRAPTOR SKELETONS ALSO SHOW THAT THIS DINOSAUR HAD A WISHBONE, A TRAIT DISTINCTIVE OF MODERN BIRDS.

Despite its smaller size, *Velociraptor* did have a comparatively large brain. It may have even been one of the smartest dinosaurs.

HOW BIG WAS VELOCIRAPTOR MONGOLIENSIS?

4 FEET
(1.2 METERS)

Velociraptor mongoliensis

7 FEET (2.1 METERS)

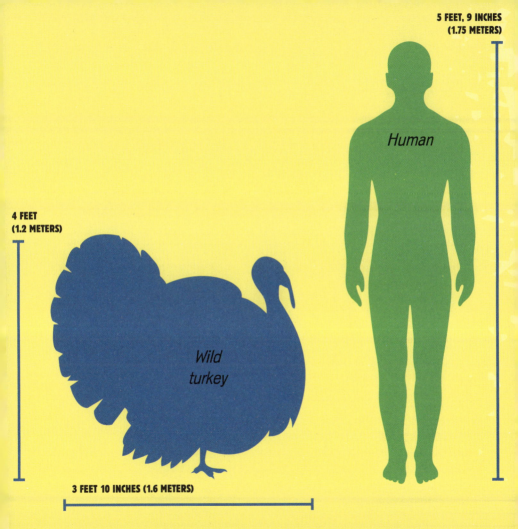

DSUNGARIPTERUS WEII

PRONUNCIATION: JUNG-gar-IP-ter-us

SIZE: A wingspan of almost 10 feet (3 meters)

LIVED: About 130 million years ago

PHYSICAL PROFILE: This pterosaur had a low crest running down the top of its skull and an upturned, toothy beak.

LARGE WINGS AREN'T NECESSARILY GRACEFUL. SCIENTISTS THINK THAT *DSUNGARIPTERUS* WOULD HAVE LANDED PRETTY ABRUPTLY WHEN IT CAME OUT OF THE AIR. THIS WOULD HAVE ALSO MEANT LOTS OF WING FLAPPING TO GET ITS BALANCE.

This flying reptile soared through the air on wings of skin extended on extremely long fourth fingers, and may have been covered by a coat of insulating fuzz.

Despite its large wingspan, *Dsungaripterus* had a sturdy, stout skeleton. This suggests it spent more of its time on land than in the air.

DINOSAURS WERE HARDLY THE ONLY CARNIVORES OF THE MESOZOIC ERA. THEIR COUSINS, THE PTEROSAURS, WERE ALSO MAJOR PREDATORS OF THE TIME.

Since the first discovery, scientists have found a number of *Dsungaripterus* fossils, including an almost complete skull.

DSUNGARIPTERUS FOSSILS WERE FOUND IN CHINA IN AN AREA CALLED THE JUNGGAR BASIN.

Wondering how *Dsungaripterus* got its name? Based on its spelling, it might not be clear why it was named, but if you look at the pronunciation, "jung-gar," it's clear that it's a reference to the area where this creature was first discovered.

HAVE YOU EVER SEEN A POLE-VAULTER FLY THROUGH THE AIR? DSUNGARIPTERUS AND OTHER PTEROSAURS TOOK OFF WITH A POLE-VAULT MOVE, PUSHING OFF THE GROUND WITH THEIR ARMS AND THROWING THEIR WINGS OPEN TO START FLAPPING INTO THE AIR.

Compared to the size of its body, the head and neck of *Dsungaripterus* was very large. Combined, the head and neck were probably about 3 feet (1 meter) long.

DSUNGARIPTERUS LIKELY HAD A BONY CREST ALONG ITS HEAD THAT RAN FROM THE BASE OF ITS SKULL HALFWAY DOWN ITS BEAK.

The last of the pterosaurs had pointed, toothless beaks, but many species also had teeth suited to different diets.

ALTHOUGH SOME PTEROSAURS HAD POINTED TEETH USEFUL FOR TRAPPING INSECTS AND SMALL FISH, FOR EXAMPLE, SPECIES LIKE DSUNGARIPTERUS HAD FLAT, CRUSHING TEETH AT THE BACK OF THEIR JAWS.

Dsungaripterus was somewhere in the middle of teeth and no teeth. At the front of its jaw, *Dsungaripterus* had no teeth and a long, pointed jaw. But at the back of its jaw, it did have some teeth!

THE COMBINATION OF POINTED BEAK AND TEETH IN THE BACK HELPED DSUNGARIPTERUS TO CRACK THE SHELLS OF INVERTEBRATES THAT LIVED INSIDE COILED SHELLS, LIKE AMMONITES, ANCIENT COUSINS OF OCTOPUS AND SQUID.

MICRORAPTOR GUI

PRONUNCIATION: MY-crow-RAP-tor

SIZE: Up to 4 feet (1.2 meters) long

LIVED: Between 125 and 120 million years ago

PHYSICAL PROFILE: This raven-size dinosaur had long feathers on its arms, legs, and at the end of its tail, which allowed it to fly in a way much like birds today.

Scientists have found a number of well-preserved *Microraptor* fossils in an area of China called the Jiufotang Formation.

IN 2015, A MICRORAPTOR FOSSIL WAS ILLEGALLY BROUGHT OVER TO THE U.S. AND PUT ON DISPLAY. ONCE AUTHORITIES LEARNED ABOUT THE ILLEGAL FOSSIL, WHICH WAS SMUGGLED IN AS A "REPLICA," IT WAS QUICKLY RETURNED TO ITS TRUE HOME IN CHINA.

Microraptor fossils are in a few different museums, but you might not see many in the United States.

The *micro* part of *microraptor* means "small," and though this creature was certainly smaller than other dinosaurs at the time, it was no less fierce.

THERE ARE TECHNICALLY THREE DIFFERENT SPECIES OF *MICRORAPTOR*, BUT SCIENTISTS WONDER WHETHER THEY SHOULD ACTUALLY ALL BE CLASSIFIED AS THE SAME SPECIES.

Microraptor was one of the most common dinosaurs in its habitat, and more than 300 fossil specimens have been discovered.

ALONG WITH THE FEATHERS ON ITS ARMS AND LEGS, *MICRORAPTOR* ALSO HAD FEATHERS ON ITS TAIL.

Scientists know that the feathers on their legs weren't just for warmth or show because of their asymmetrical shape, which is common for feathers adapted for flight.

WHEN YOU HEAR *MICRORAPTOR* HAD WINGS, YOU MIGHT PICTURE TWO, BUT IT ACTUALLY HAD GROUPS OF FEATHERS ON BOTH ITS ARMS AND LEGS, GIVING IT THE APPEARANCE OF HAVING FOUR SEPARATE WINGS.

MICRORAPTOR MAY NOT HAVE BEEN ABLE TO TRULY FLY VERY FAR, BUT IT MAY HAVE GLIDED DOWN FROM TREES USING ALL FOUR LIMBS EXTENDED TO THE SIDES.

How do scientists know? They actually tested it! Using models in a wind tunnel, they were able to learn how *Microraptor* could have used its limbs to glide.

THE WAY *MICRORAPTOR* COULD HAVE FLOWN HAS BEEN COMPARED TO EARLY BIPLANES. OLDER PLANES USED TO HAVE FOUR WINGS, TWO ON EACH SIDE. JUST LIKE AIRPLANES, WHICH NOW HAVE JUST TWO WINGS, THE BACK TWO WINGS ON PREHISTORIC BIRDS EVENTUALLY BECAME UNNECESSARY.

Gut contents in *Microraptor* skeletons have shown that this dinosaur often ate small prey such as shrewlike mammals and early birds.

SINORNITHOSAURUS MILLENII

PRONUNCIATION: SINE-or-NITH-o-SAWR-us

The feathered *Sinornithosaurus* was one of the smallest creatures in a family of dinosaurs called *Dromaeosauridae*.

SIZE: About 3 feet (1 meter) long

LIVED: About 124 million years ago

PHYSICAL PROFILE: A small raptor dinosaur, covered in feathers, with a highly extendable claw on each foot

From the anatomy of its eyes, paleontologists expect that *Sinornithosaurus* hunted from dawn to dusk at short intervals.

Because these fossils were preserved so well in sediment of the region, scientists were able to find evidence of feathers by looking at the impressions on its bones.

Deeper studies of *Sinornithosaurus* cells found in the fossils show that its feathers had different colors.

SINORNITHOSAURUS HAD TWO TYPES OF FEATHERS: ONE TYPE WERE DOWN-LIKE FEATHERS JOINED TOGETHER IN SMALL TUFTS, WHICH COULD HAVE BEEN FOR WARMTH, AND THE SECOND TYPE WERE FEATHERS LIKE YOU SEE ON MODERN BIRDS.

Sinornithosaurus might sound like a mouthful, but it's actually a combination of Latin and Greek words that means "Chinese bird-lizard," and that's exactly what this raptor covered in feathers and found in the Yixian Formation of China was.

Sinornithosaurus feathers may have looked like bird feathers in appearance but based on studies scientists think that they weren't adapted for flying.

SCIENTISTS SPECULATE THAT *SINORNITHOSAURUS* COULD PROBABLY HAVE GLIDED FOR SHORT DISTANCES FROM TREES.

Have you ever flapped your arms to pretend to fly? By studying its shoulder blades, scientists have learned that *Sinornithosaurus* may have been able to flap its arms like a bird, making the theory that they could glide more likely.

IN 2012, SCIENTISTS STUDIED *SINORNITHOSAURUS* FEATHERS AND LEARNED THAT THEY WOULD HAVE BEEN DIFFERENT COLORS ON DIFFERENT PARTS OF ITS BODY, INCLUDING REDDISH-BROWN, YELLOW, BLACK, AND GRAY.

Unlike *Dilophosaurus wetherilli* (see page 74), *Sinornithosaurus* actually may have been venomous, and it was the first species of venomous dinosaur identified.

SINORNITHOSAURUS HAD MIDDLE TEETH THAT WERE INCREDIBLY LONG AND FANGLIKE WITH GROOVES ON THE SURFACE THAT ARE OFTEN FOUND IN VENOMOUS ANIMALS.

Sinornithosaurus was a hunter and may have attacked small birds by piercing its prey with its sharp fangs and injecting venom that would stun the prey.

DOES THIS HUNTING STYLE SOUND FAMILIAR? SINORNITHOSAURUS HAS ACTUALLY BEEN COMPARED TO MODERN SNAKES, WHICH HUNT IN A SIMILAR WAY.

Some scientists question whether *Sinornithosaurus* was truly venomous, saying that the shape of its teeth alone can't prove that it would have been able to produce venom.

LIKE OTHER RAPTORS, SINORNITHOSAURUS HARD SHARP, EFFECTIVE CLAWS THAT WOULD HAVE BEEN HELPFUL FOR CATCHING PREY.

SUCHOMIMUS TENERENSIS

PRONUNCIATION: SOOK-o-MIME-us

SIZE: About 30 feet (9 meters) long

LIVED: Between 121 and 113 million years ago

PHYSICAL PROFILE: A large predatory dinosaur with thick, grasping claws on the hands, a low sail on its back, and a very long snout that gave this "crocodile mimic" its name

THE NAME *SUCHOMIMUS* MEANS "CROCODILE MIMIC," AND YOU MIGHT NOTICE SOME PHYSICAL SIMILARITIES BETWEEN *SUCHOMIMUS* AND MODERN CROCODILES.

The biggest similarity between *Suchomimus* and modern crocodiles may be the shape of their skulls. *Suchomimus* had a crocodile-like skull shape. It had a long snout and lower jaw with lots of long, thin teeth.

IN FACT, IT MAY HAVE HAD AROUND 100 OF THOSE THIN TEETH, WHICH WERE SLIGHTLY CURVED IN SHAPE LIKE A FISHING HOOK.

Those teeth might not look powerful like the giant ones of other dinosaurs of the time, but they were especially helpful for catching prey like fish that would have been slippery.

FOSSILS FOND IN AFRICA SUGGEST THAT THIS CREATURE LIVED AROUND RIVERS AND LAGOONS WHERE BOTH LAND AND WATER WERE AVAILABLE, MUCH LIKE MODERN CROCODILES.

Suchomimus would have been adapted to hunt prey in both water and on land. It didn't just eat fish. *Suchomimus* likely also fed on small dinosaurs and birds. Because its teeth were best for catching, not killing prey, it may have looked for smaller creatures or scaveneged for animals that were already dead.

SUCHOMIMUS ALSO HAD LARGE CLAWS THAT WOULD HAVE HELPED IT TO CATCH AND HOLD PREY.

The *Suchomimus* fossils scientists have found were not in very good shape when they were discovered, which means that there's still a lot for scientists to learn about this creature.

FOSSILS SHOW THAT *SUCHOMIMUS* HAD AN ENLARGED SPINE ON ITS BACK. SCIENTISTS THINK THESE SPINES WOULD HAVE HELD UP A HUMPLIKE SAIL OF SKIN.

No one knows why *Suchomimus* had a sail on its back. If you grow up to be a paleontologist, maybe you'll find out!

THE LONG-SNOUTED *SUCHOMIMUS* COULD HAVE HUNTED A BABY *SARCOSUCHUS IMPERATOR*—A CROCODILE THAT COULD GROW UP TO 40 FEET (12 METERS) LONG IF IT SURVIVED TO ADULTHOOD.

Fossils of similar creatures have been found in Europe and South America, but because their habitats are so different and far apart, they were likely different species.

FOSSILS INDICATE THAT *SUCHOMIMUS* COULD HAVE WEIGHED BETWEEN 5,000 AND 10,000 POUNDS (2,268 TO 4,536 KILOGRAMS), AND SCIENTISTS SUSPECT THAT THOSE FOSSILS MAY NOT HAVE EVEN BEEN FULLY GROWN ADULTS!

KRYPTOPS PALAIOS

PRONUNCIATION: CRYP-tops

SIZE: About 20 feet (6 meters) long

LIVED: 110 million years ago

PHYSICAL PROFILE: This stout carnivore had small, weak arms and a short, deep skull that gave it a bulldog-like appearance.

HAVE YOU EVER WORN A MASK? BASED ON THE BLOOD VESSELS AND GROOVES ON ITS UPPER JAWBONES, PALEONTOLOGISTS SUSPECT THAT *KRYPTOPS* HAD SOME KIND OF TOUGH, ROUGH FACIAL COVERING.

- - - - - - - - - - - - - - - - - - - -

The name *Kryptops* is actually a reference to this theory, because it means "covered face."

- - - - - - - - - - - - - - - - - - - -

KRYPTOPS MAY HAVE PREYED ON DINOSAURS LIKE *NIGERSAURUS TAQUETI*, *OURANOSAURUS NIGERIENSIS*, AND *LURDUSAURUS ARENATUS*.

- - - - - - - - - - - - - - - - - - - -

Scientists have only discovered partial fossils of *Kryptops*, and these were found very far apart from one another. This makes it difficult to tell exactly which fossils belonged to *Kryptops* and which belonged to other unidentified animals in the area.

- - - - - - - - - - - - - - - - - - - -

SCIENTISTS HAVE COMPARED DISCOVERIES OF *KRYPTOPS* FOSSILS TO SIMILAR FOSSILS IN SOUTH AMERICA, INDIA, AND MADAGASCAR TO BETTER UNDERSTAND HOW THE LANDMASSES MOVED FARTHER AWAY FROM ONE ANOTHER. THE SIMILAR, BUT NOT EXACT, FOSSILS LED SCIENTISTS TO BELIEVE THAT THE LANDMASSES HAD STARTED TO MOVE APART FROM ONE ANOTHER, BUT THEY MAY HAVE NOT BEEN ENTIRELY SEPARATE YET.

- - - - - - - - - - - - - - - - - - - -

This masked, carnivorous creature was likely both a hunter and a scavenger.

- - - - - - - - - - - - - - - - - - - -

FOSSILS OF *KRYPTOPS* HAVE BEEN FOUND IN AN AREA OF AFRICA CALLED THE ELRHAZ FORMATION.

ACROCANTHOSAURUS ATOKENSIS

PRONUNCIATION: AK-ro-KANTH-uh-SAWR-us

No dinosaur was safe from the terrifying *Acrocanthosaurus*. It would have preyed on ornithopods and ankylosaurs alike.

Despite its massive size, *Acrocanthosaurus* still walked upright on two feet rather than on all fours.

Other dinosaurs at the time, like *Spinosaurus aegyptiacus* (see page 150), had similar large spines, but scientists aren't sure how, or if, they are related.

During the early part of the Cretaceous period, cousins of *Allosaurus fragilis* (see page 70) were the biggest, baddest carnivores around. Among the most imposing was *Acrocanthosaurus*.

Along its back, *Acrocanthosaurus* had tall spines, some over a foot (0.3 meters) tall, that led to its name, which means "high-spined lizard."

The spines would have held up a large sail that ran along its neck, back, and tail.

SIZE: Up to 40 feet (12 meters) long and 6 tons (5.4 metric tons)

LIVED: About 110 million years ago

PHYSICAL PROFILE: A huge carnivore with a large skull set with knifelike teeth, three-clawed arms, and a high, prominent ridge running along its back.

FOSSILS FOUND IN NORTH AMERICA SHOW THAT THIS CARNIVORE WOULD HAVE BEEN THE LARGEST IN THE FAMILY OF ANIMALS CALLED CARCHARODONTOSAURIDAE, AND IT WAS ALSO ONE OF THE LARGEST CARNIVORES IN ALL OF NORTH AMERICA AT THE TIME.

The first fossils of *Acrocanthosaurus* were found in the deserts of modern-day Oklahoma. The fossils may have been found as early as the 1940s, but didn't get much attention until more fossils started popping up.

SINCE *ACROCANTHOSAURUS* WAS FIRST DISCOVERED, SEVERAL MORE SPECIMENS HAVE BEEN FOUND ALL ACROSS AMERICA, INCLUDING SITES IN OKLAHOMA, TEXAS, WYOMING, ARIZONA, AND EVEN MARYLAND. ONE OF THE FOSSILS FOUND WAS AN ALMOST COMPLETE SKULL, A RARE FIND FOR PALEONTOLOGISTS.

Scientists aren't exactly sure why *Acrocanthosaurus* had a sail. It may have been to help regulate its temperature. Or, the sail could have helped it to appear even larger and more intimidating, scaring off potential rivals.

THIS HUGE, HEAVY DINOSAUR COULD HAVE WEIGHED ANYWHERE FROM 6,000 TO 10,000 POUNDS (2,722 TO 4,536 KILOGRAMS) AS AN ADULT.

ACROCANTHOSAURUS ARM ANATOMY SUGGESTS THIS CARNIVORE COULD DIG ITS LARGE CLAWS INTO PREY AND HOLD VICTIMS CLOSE WHILE DELIVERING A FATAL BITE. IN OTHER WORDS, ITS HUGS WERE DEADLY.

A curious trackway found in Texas might even show this predator in action. The main trackway preserves the pothole-like footsteps of a long-necked, heavy-bodied sauropod dinosaur. The tracks of a very large predator—likely *Acrocanthosaurus* or a close relative—come in from the side and collide with those of the giant herbivore.

WHAT DOES THIS MEAN? PERHAPS THE ACROCANTHOSAURUS WAS STALKING ITS PREY FROM A DISTANCE, FOLLOWING IT UNTIL JUST THE RIGHT MOMENT. OR MAYBE THE TRACKS RECORD AN ATTACK.

Some paleontologists point to a missing *Acrocanthosaurus* track as the moment when the carnivore bit the sauropod and was lifted off its feet. Either way, being followed by an *Acrocanthosaurus* must have been a chilling experience.

TRUE OR FALSE

1. T/F BECAUSE *VELOCIRAPTOR MONGOLIENSIS* HAD FEATHERS AND WINGS, IT COULD FLY.

2. T/F *DSUNGARIPTERUS WEII* WAS A PTEROSAUR, WHICH MEANS IT WAS A FLYING REPTILE.

3. T / F INSTEAD OF TWO WINGS, *MICRORAPTOR GUI* HAD FOUR WINGS IT USED TO GLIDE THROUGH THE AIR.

4. T / F *SUCHOMIMUS TENERENSIS* HAD ABOUT 100 TEETH.

5. T / F *KRYPTOPS PALAIOS* LIKELY HAD SOME KIND OF TOUGH FACIAL COVERING.

ANSWERS: 1. F; 2. T; 3. T; 4. T; 5. T

DELTADROMEUS AGILIS

PRONUNCIATION: DEL-ta-DRO-me-us

Deltadromeus fossils have been found in areas of northern Africa.

SIZE: About 26 feet (8 meters) long

LIVED: Around 95 million years ago

PHYSICAL PROFILE: A medium-sized, slender carnivore with long legs for its size

The hind legs of *Deltadromeus* were especially long and slender, meaning it would have likely been a fast runner.

ITS NAME ALSO SUGGESTS ITS RUNNING PROWESS, AS *DELTADROMEUS* MEANS "DELTA RUNNER."

Fast legs would have been especially helpful in the dangerous habitat where *Deltadromeus* lived. At about 26 feet (8 meters) long, it was a midsized creature compared to other dinosaurs.

THOSE LITTLE LEGS STILL HAD TO HOLD UP PLENTY OF WEIGHT. *DELTADROMEUS* WOULD HAVE CLOCKED IN SOMEWHERE OVER 2,000 POUNDS (907 KILOGRAMS).

Deltadromeus was likely a carnivore, but it would have had stiff competition for food, as it lived in the same place and at the same time as the bigger predators like *Spinosaurus aegyptiacus* (see page 150).

SCIENTISTS HAVE ONLY FOUND LIMITED *DELTADROMEUS* FOSSILS, AND THEY DON'T HAVE A COMPLETE SKELETON. THIS HAS LED TO SOME SPECULATION THAT *DELTADROMEUS* MAY ACTUALLY BE A YOUNG FORM OF ANOTHER SPECIES OF DINOSAUR.

In fact, the fossils were originally thought to be *Bahariasaurus ingens* bones, but there were too many differences to confirm them as part of that species, so *Deltadromeus* was identified as its own type.

SCIENTISTS MAY HAVE UNCOVERED SOME *DELTADROMEUS* TEETH, BUT NO SKULL FOSSILS HAVE EVER BEEN FOUND.

Although similar fossils have been recovered in South America, the fossils there were likely a different species because they lived so far away.

SPINOSAURUS AEGYPTIACUS

PRONUNCIATION: SPY-no-SAWR-us

Spinosaurus was likely the biggest of the Cretaceous carnivores in its habitat.

SIZE: About 45 feet (13.7 meters) long

LIVED: Between 112 and 97 million years ago

PHYSICAL PROFILE: A huge, sail-backed carnivore with a long, low skull full of conical teeth

The name *Spinosaurus* comes from the giant spines growing out of its back that could reach up to 7 feet (2 meters) long! They likely held up a skinlike sail on its back.

LOCATION IS EVERYTHING. THERE ARE TWO DIFFERENT SPECIES OF *SPINOSAURUS* THAT ARE NAMED BASED ON WHERE THEY WERE FOUND. *SPINOSAURUS AEGYPTIACUS* WAS DISCOVERED IN MODERN-DAY EGYPT, WHILE THE SIMILAR *SPINOSAURUS MAROCCANUS* LIVED IN MODERN-DAY MOROCCO.

With its massive sail, *Spinosaurus* would easily have looked doubly as large as it actually was.

Based on its anatomy, *Spinosaurus* would have had its weight shifted slightly forward. Although this would have helped it to swim, it also means that *Spinosaurus* would likely have walked on all fours when it was on land.

SPINOSAURUS WAS LARGER IN SIZE THAN EVEN THE LATER *TYRANNOSAURUS REX* (SEE PAGE 230)!

Fossils have been found in North Africa, where the habitat may have been swampy.

SPINOSAURUS HAD VERY DENSE BONES, WHICH MAY HAVE ACTED LIKE BALLAST TO HELP KEEP THE DINOSAUR SUBMERGED WHEN IT WENT HUNTING IN LAKES AND RIVERS.

It also had short hind limbs, a trait common in early ancestors of whales and other water-dwelling animals.

ITS WIDE, CLAWED FEET WOULD HAVE BEEN USEFUL TO HELP *SPINOSAURUS* PADDLE IN THE WATER.

Spinosaurus was undoubtedly a carnivore. It had a long snout and sharp teeth that could have helped it to catch fish as prey.

SPINOSAURUS MAY HAVE ADAPTED TO A WATERY ENVIRONMENT. SCIENTISTS THINK IT MAY HAVE BEEN ONE OF THE FIRST TRUE DINOSAURS THAT WAS ABLE TO SWIM. IT MAY HAVE EVEN SPENT A GOOD PORTION OF ITS LIFE IN THE WATER!

Although scientists think the Sahara could be filled with *Spinosaurus* fossils, it's also a very harsh environment, making those fossils very difficult to find.

SPINOSAURUS HAS A PRETTY LITERAL NAME: "SPINE LIZARD."

ALTHOUGH SCIENTISTS KNOW THAT *SPINOSAURUS* HAD A LARGE SAIL, THEY'RE NOT EXACTLY SURE WHY. IT COULD HAVE BEEN TO WARD OFF ENEMIES, BUT EVEN WITHOUT THE SAIL THIS DINOSAUR WAS ONE OF THE LARGEST IN THE LAND.

Studying its spine has shown scientists that the vertebrae were somewhat flexible, meaning *Spinosaurus* could probably have arched its back. This may have allowed it to spread the sail even farther.

OTHER THEORIES ABOUT THE PURPOSE OF THE SAIL ARE THAT IT WAS FOR TEMPERATURE REGULATION OR MATING. MOST LIKELY, THE SAIL WAS JUST FOR DISPLAY.

Scientists can't be sure, but they think the sail may have been brightly colored like some modern-day reptiles. If that's the case, then the theory that the sail was for display is most likely.

BECAUSE THEY DON'T HAVE A COMPLETE SET OF FOSSILS, SCIENTISTS AREN'T SURE EXACTLY HOW BIG *SPINOSAURUS* WAS. IT MAY HAVE BEEN EVEN LARGER THAN THEY CURRENTLY THINK!

You won't find the original fossils in any museum. The remains were lost during the bombings of World War II. Thank goodness, the scientist who discovered them kept incredibly detailed notes, including lots of descriptions and sketches.

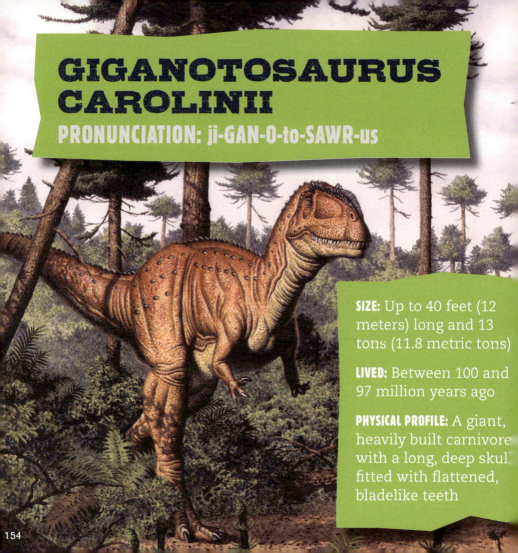

GIGANOTOSAURUS CAROLINII

PRONUNCIATION: ji-GAN-O-to-SAWR-us

SIZE: Up to 40 feet (12 meters) long and 13 tons (11.8 metric tons)

LIVED: Between 100 and 97 million years ago

PHYSICAL PROFILE: A giant, heavily built carnivore with a long, deep skull fitted with flattened, bladelike teeth

THIS HEFTY DINOSAUR COULD HAVE WEIGHED ANYWHERE FROM 13,000 TO 17,000 POUNDS (5,897 TO 7,711 KILOGRAMS)! SOME SCIENTISTS EVEN THINK THAT *GIGANOTOSAURUS* COULD HAVE WEIGHED A LOT MORE.

GIGANOTOSAURUS WAS ANOTHER OF THE LARGEST CARNIVOROUS DINOSAURS, ABOUT THE SAME SIZE OR SLIGHTLY LARGER THAN TYRANNOSAURUS REX (SEE PAGE 230).

Tyrannosaurus and *Giganotosaurus* wouldn't have been in any competition, though. *Giganotosaurus* lived in modern-day Argentina, and it was alive about 30 million years before *Tyrannosaurus*.

THE NAME *GIGANOTOSAURUS* MEANS "GIANT SOUTHERN LIZARD," THANKS TO ITS SIZE AND HABITAT.

Giganotosaurus was a member of the dinosaur family Carcharodontosauridae. The family is known for having sharp, sharklike teeth.

GIGANOTOSAURUS WAS A BIPEDAL DINOSAUR THAT WALKED UPRIGHT ON ITS POWERFUL HIND LEGS.

Despite its size, *Giganotosaurus* could have been pretty quick and agile. It had a thin, pointed tail that would have been useful for balancing and making quick turns while it ran.

SOME SCIENTISTS THINK *GIGANOTOSAURUS* MAY HAVE BEEN ABLE TO RUN AS FAST AS 30 MILES (48 KILOMETERS) PER HOUR!

Giganotosaurus had three fingers on each arm and incredibly sharp claws.

THE FOSSILS OF *GIGANOTOSAURUS* ARMS ARE INCOMPLETE AND NOT VERY WELL PRESERVED, SO SCIENTISTS AREN'T SURE EXACTLY HOW POWERFUL ITS ARMS WERE.

Giganotosaurus had a massive skull. One skull fossil measured a little over 5 feet (1.5 meters) long!

BASED ON RESEARCH INTO THE SIZE OF ITS SKULL, SCIENTISTS THINK *GIGANOTOSAURUS* PROBABLY HAD A PRETTY SMALL BRAIN, ESPECIALLY WHEN COMPARED TO THE THEORIZED BRAIN SIZE OF *TYRANNOSAURUS*.

Inside that skull, *Giganotosaurus* had flat, serrated teeth that are pretty typical for carnivores.

BASED ON ITS SIZE, *GIGANOTOSAURUS* LIKELY WASN'T ANYONE'S PREY, BUT IT WAS A PREDATOR THAT HUNTED MANY OTHER LARGE, HERBIVOROUS DINOSAURS.

The first discovery of *Giganotosaurus* in 1993 revealed a skeleton that was about 70 percent complete. Scientists still do not have a full skeleton.

THE FIRST FOSSILS WERE ACTUALLY DISCOVERED BY AN AMATEUR DINOSAUR HUNTER NAMED RUBÉN DARIO CAROLINI. WHEN PALEONTOLOGISTS STUDIED THE *GIGANOTOSAURUS*, THEY GAVE IT THE SPECIES NAME *CAROLINII* TO HONOR THE DISCOVERER.

So far, remains of only two different *Giganotosaurus* speciment have been found. That means that there's still a lot to learn about *Giganotosaurus* and how it grew and lived!

EKRIXINATOSAURUS NOVASI

PRONUNCIATION: EK-rix-IN-at-o-SAWR-us

SIZE: About 25 feet (7.6 meters) long

LIVED: Between 100 and 97 million years ago

PHYSICAL PROFILE: Large carnivore with a short, deep skull and tiny arms (center)

Fossils of the carnivorous *Ekrixinatosaurus* have been found in Argentina, including some partial skull remains.

IN THE CASE OF DINOSAURS, SIZE MATTERS! BASED ON ITS LARGE SIZE, *EKRIXINATOSAURUS* LIKELY PREYED ON OTHER LARGE DINOSAURS IN ITS HABITAT.

However, *Ekrixinatosaurus* was neither the biggest nor the most terrifying dinosaur on the block. Fossils of the terrifying *Giganotosaurus carolinii* (see page 154) were found in the same area as *Ekrixinatosaurus*.

CAN YOU IMAGINE COMING ACROSS A FOSSIL IN YOUR OWN BACKYARD? FOSSILS OF *EKRIXINATOSAURUS* WERE FOUND ENTIRELY BY ACCIDENT. CONSTRUCTION TO BUILD A GAS PIPELINE REVEALED THE REMAINS IN 2004.

The discovery yielded a partial skeleton, allowing paleontologists to identify *Ekrixinatosaurus* as an entirely new species. But this first discovery is still one of the only *Ekrixinatosaurus* fossils found.

EKRIXINATOSAURUS HAD JAWS THAT CURVED SLIGHTLY UPWARD.

The size of its skull and limbs in proportion to its body suggest that this sturdy animal could hold its own in a fight.

WHY *EKRIXINATOSAURUS* AND ITS CLOSE RELATIVES HAD SUCH SMALL ARMS IS A MYSTERY, BUT THE MUSCLE ATTACHMENTS ON ITS BONES HINT THAT THEY WERE STILL USEFUL FOR SOMETHING.

By examining its skull, scientists have determined that *Ekrixinatosaurus* was likely covered in wrinkled skin.

EOCARCHARIA DINOPS
PRONUNCIATION: EE-o-CAR-char-EE-ah

SIZE: About 25 feet (7.6 meters) long

LIVED: 110 million years ago

PHYSICAL PROFILE: A midsize predator with a long, deep skull full of knife-shaped teeth that give this "dawn shark" dinosaur its name

Don't let the name of this creature fool you. *Eocarcharia* means "dawn shark," but this creature was absolutely a dinosaur, not a shark.

ITS NAME COMES FROM ITS SHARKLIKE TEETH. *EOCARCHARIA* HAD SERRATED, SLICING TEETH THAT WERE LIKELY AS POWERFUL AS ANY SHARK'S TEETH.

This dinosaur wasn't an early riser. "Dawn" is actually a reference to it being one of the earlier dinosaurs with these traits.

EOCARCHARIA IS PART OF THE FAMILY CARCHARODONTOSAURIDAE, WHICH IS KNOWN FOR HAVING SHARKLIKE TEETH

These teeth undoubtedly meant that *Eocarcharia* was a carnivore.

A ROUGH RIDGE OF BONE ON THIS DINOSAUR'S BROW IS WHY PALEONTOLOGISTS GAVE IT THE SPECIES NAME *DINOPS*, MEANING "FIERCE-EYED."

Scienstists aren't sure exactly why it had the facial ridge. One theory is that it was just for display.

IN FACT, SCIENTISTS SPECULATE THAT THE RIDGE MAY HAVE BEEN A DIFFERENT COLOR THAN THE REST OF THE HEAD.

Fossils found in the Elrhaz formation suggest that *Eocarcharia* inhabited what is now Africa, especially around Niger.

SAUROPOSEIDON PROTELES

PRONUNCIATION: SORE-o-poe-PSY-don

SIZE: Between 89 and 112 feet (27 to 34 meters) long

LIVED: About 110 million years ago

PHYSICAL PROFILE: One of the last North American sauropod dinosaurs, *Sauroposeidon* walked on all fours and had an incredibly long neck.

Sauroposeidon fossils have been uncovered in modern-day Oklahoma and Texas.

Unlike in the Jurassic period, by the Cretaceous period most of the massive sauropod dinosaurs with their long necks and long tails had died out, but *Sauroposeidon* was an exception.

EVEN COMPARED TO OTHER SAUROPODS, *SAUROPOSEIDON* HAD AN OUTRAGEOUSLY LONG NECK. SCIENTISTS THINK THAT IF IT STOOD UP STRAIGHT, THIS DINOSAUR WOULD HAVE BEEN MORE THAN 56 FEET (17 METERS) TALL!

Did you know that even wood can turn into fossils? One type of fossil, called petrified wood, occurs when ancient wood slowly turns to stone. The fossils of *Sauroposeidon* were so unusual that when they were first discovered in 1994, scientists thought they might be petrified wood instead of bones from a real creature.

HAVE YOU EVER HEARD OF THE GREEK GODS? THE NAME *SAUROPOSEIDON* IS ACTUALLY A REFERENCE TO THE GREEK GOD POSEIDON, WHO WAS ASSOCIATED WITH THE SEA AND EARTHQUAKES.

Texas loves this unique dinosaur so much that it's their official state dinosaur!

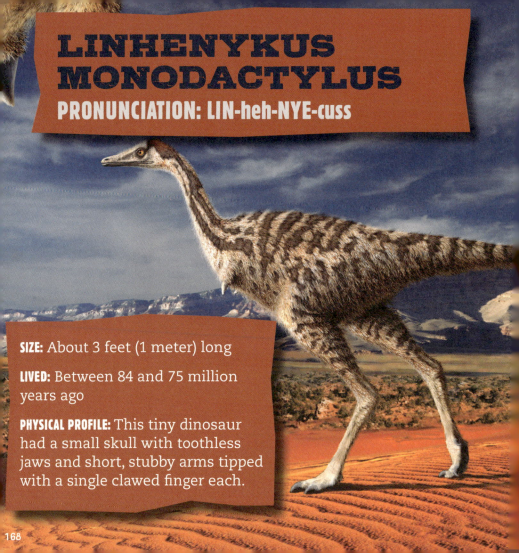

LINHENYKUS MONODACTYLUS
PRONUNCIATION: LIN-heh-NYE-cuss

SIZE: About 3 feet (1 meter) long

LIVED: Between 84 and 75 million years ago

PHYSICAL PROFILE: This tiny dinosaur had a small skull with toothless jaws and short, stubby arms tipped with a single clawed finger each.

The first *Linhenykus* fossils were found in Mongolia, and it gets its name from the nearby city of Linhe.

LINHENYKUS AND ITS CLOSE RELATIVES WERE SMALL DINOSAURS WITH SHORT, STOUT HAND CLAWS AND FEW OR NO TEETH IN THEIR MOUTHS.

You might not want to eat bugs, but *Linhenykus* did. Paleontologists think *Linhenykus*, because of its lack of teeth, was the dinosaur equivalent of an anteater. That means that it would have eaten insects. Paleontologists have found termite nests in petrified wood going back to the Jurassic period, and insects like bees were evolving in the early Cretaceous period, so it's no surprise that some dinosaurs evolved to dine on this new source of crunchy insect food!

LINHENYKUS HAD SHORT, HEAVILY BUILT FOREARMS.

Linhenykus didn't just have short arms. This little dinosaur only had one finger on each hand!

MUCH LIKE MODERN ANTEATERS, IT MIGHT HAVE USED ITS CLAWS TO DIG FOR INSECTS TO EAT.

When *Linhenykus* was first discovered, those fingers made it one of the most unusual dinosaurs found, but eventually it was discovered that a whole family of dinosaurs called alvarezsaurs relied heavily on one claw.

MOST OTHER ALVAREZSAURS HAD SECOND OR THIRD FINGERS THAT WEREN'T FUNCTIONAL, BUT LINHENYKUS WAS UNIQUE BECAUSE IT TRULY ONLY HAD ONE.

DINO QUIZ

1. HOW TALL COULD THE SPINES OF SPINOSAURUS AEGYPTIACUS GROW?

A. 1 FOOT (0.3 METERS)   C. 5 FEET (1.5 METERS)

B. 3 FEET (1 METER)   D. 7 FEET (2 METERS)

2. WHICH LARGE PREDATOR COULD RUN AT ABOUT 30 MILES (48 KILOMETERS) PER HOUR?

A. SPINOSAURUS AEGYPTIACUS

B. GIGANOTOSAURUS CAROLINII

C. EOCARCHARIA DINOPS

D. LINHENYKUS MONODACTYLUS

3. WHAT *EKRIXINATOSAURUS NOVASI* FOSSIL DID SCIENTISTS STUDY TO LEARN ABOUT ITS SKIN?

A. SKULL

B. SPINE

C. TAIL

D. LEG

4. WHAT DID THE NAME *EOCARCHARIA DINOPS* MEAN?

A. DAWN WHALE

B. NIGHT WHALE

C. DAWN SHARK

D. NIGHT SHARK

5. TO WHAT MODERN ANIMAL HAS *LINHENYKUS MONODACTYLUS* BEEN COMPARED?

A. AARDVARK

B. ARMADILLO

C. ANACONDA

D. ANTEATER

Answers: 1. D; 2. B; 3. A; 4. C; 5. D

LINHERAPTOR EXQUISITUS
PRONUNCIATION: LIN-heh-RAP-tor

At just 7 feet (2 meters) long and about 55 pounds (25 kilograms), this light predator would have been quick and agile.

SIZE: Almost 7 feet (2 meters) long

LIVED: Between 84 and 75 million years ago

PHYSICAL PROFILE: A midsize raptor dinosaur with large, grasping hands, a stiff tail, and an extendable claw on each food suited to pinning down prey

THIS RELATIVE OF THE FAMOUS *VELOCIRAPTOR MONGOLIENSIS* (SEE PAGE 118) WAS FIRST DISCOVERED IN MONGOLIA IN 2008.

Luckily for scientists, the *Linheraptor* skeleton they uncovered was incredibly well preserved in sandstone rock and nearly complete.

LINHERAPTOR WAS PART OF THE DROMAEOSAURIDAE FAMILY, WHICH MEANS THAT IT WAS UNDOUBTEDLY A CARNIVORE.

Like other members of its family, *Linheraptor* had a sharp claw on each foot known as a "killing claw" that would have helped it to trap prey.

LINHERAPTOR MOST LIKELY HUNTED SMALL, HORNED DINOSAURS THAT WERE RELATED TO *TRICERATOPS HORRIDUS* (SEE PAGE 226).

EVEN THOUGH NO FEATHERS WERE FOUND WITH THE SKELETON, WE KNOW FROM CLOSE RELATIVES THAT *LINHERAPTOR* WAS DEFINITELY A FLUFFY DINOSAUR.

Many dinosaurs, like *Linheraptor*, were covered with feathers. That might seem strange for animals that couldn't fly, but paleontologists have found that feathers first evolved for reasons other than taking to the air.

PREDATORS LIKE *LINHERAPTOR* COULD HAVE FLAPPED THEIR FEATHERY ARMS TO HELP THEM KEEP A GRIP ON TITLED SURFACES LIKE FALLEN LOGS OR TO HELP KEEP PINNED PREY FROM ESCAPING.

Paleontologists have also discovered that feathered dinosaurs often had unique color patterns and feather shapes that wouldn't have been useful for flying but would have been great for display.

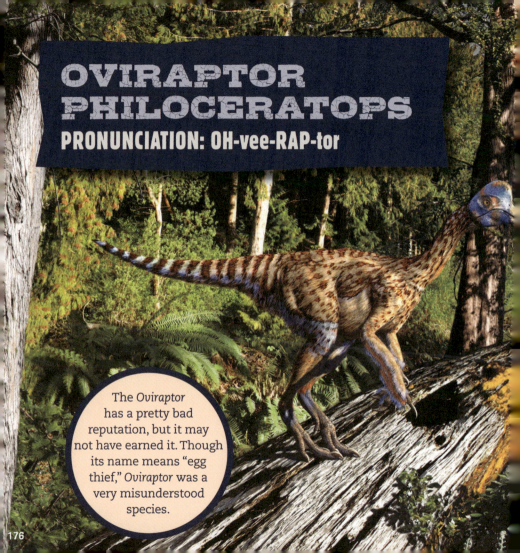

OVIRAPTOR PHILOCERATOPS
PRONUNCIATION: OH-vee-RAP-tor

The *Oviraptor* has a pretty bad reputation, but it may not have earned it. Though its name means "egg thief," *Oviraptor* was a very misunderstood species.

Anatomically, *Oviraptor* had a similar rib cage to modern birds.

Shake your tail feathers! *Oviraptor* had an interestingly flexible and muscular tail. Scientists think they may have shaken it when looking for mates.

Because so many of its relatives had feathers, scientists think *Oviraptor* was likely also a feathered dinosaur.

SIZE: About 5 feet (1.5 meters) long

LIVED: Around 75 million years ago

PHYSICAL PROFILE: A dinosaur that walked on two legs with a covering of feathers and a toothless, parrot-like beak

The first *Oviraptor* fossils were found in Mongolia near a nest of eggs, leading scientists to believe these fearsome-looking carnivores were planning to eat the eggs. Their curved upper jaw gave support to this theory, because they would have been able to easily crush eggs or shellfish.

SINCE THE FIRST DISCOVERY, MORE EVIDENCE OF *OVIRAPTOR* DYING NEAR EGGS HAS BEEN FOUND, BUT BY ANALYZING THE CONTENTS OF THE EGGS, SCIENTISTS HAVE DISCOVERED THAT MANY ACTUALLY CONTAINED *OVIRAPTOR* EMBRYO.

THAT MEANS *OVIRAPTOR* MAY NOT HAVE BEEN STEALING EGGS AT ALL. INSTEAD, IT MAY HAVE DIED WHILE BROODING EGGS IN ITS NEST TO KEEP THEM WARM.

Oviraptor had lots of birdlike similarities including its beak and a crest on top of its head.

NOT ALL PREDATORY DINOSAURS HAD BIG, SHARP TEETH. THE PARROTLIKE *OVIRAPTOR* DID NOT HAVE A TOOTH IN ITS MOUTH, YET IT WAS CAPABLE OF EATING A MIXED DIET OF BOTH GREENS AND MEAT.

Like most other dinosaurs, *Oviraptor* couldn't chew.

SOME BONES JUTTING DOWN FROM THE ROOF OF THIS DINOSAUR'S MOUTH COULD HAVE HELPED IT CRUSH SMALL MORSELS, BUT BEYOND THAT, *OVIRAPTOR* HAD TO SWALLOW EACH MOUTHFUL WHOLE.

Fortunately for this dinosaur, there were plenty of appetizers in its Cretaceous habitat. Paleontologists have found freshwater clams in the same area as *Oviraptor*, which the dinosaur could have cracked open in its beak, and one specimen of the predator was found with a small lizard inside.

TROODON FORMOSUS

PRONUNCIATION: TRO-o-DON

The first descriptions of *Troodon* date as far back as 1856, but there is some debate over the species name.

Like other raptors, *Troodon* had sharp, powerful claws on its feet.

SIZE: Almost 8 feet (2.4 meters) long

LIVED: About 77 million years ago

PHYSICAL PROFILE: A slender raptor dinosaur with small teeth, large eyes, and an extendable toe claw on each foot

Since that first discovery, scientists have found fossils from more than 20 different potential *Troodon* specimens.

Scientists think that *Troodon* may also have been covered in feathers like other members of its family.

Potential *Troodon* fossils have been found all across North America, even as far as Alberta, Canada.

Because *Troodon's* teeth are short and broad, scientists think it may have adapted to eat both plants and prey, making it an omnivore.

Although not exactly the same species as *Troodon*, fossils of closely related dinosaurs have also been found in Asia.

This small predator would have walked on two legs and used its arms to graps prey. Each of its arms had three fingers for grasping.

WHEN *TROODON* WAS FIRST DISCOVERED, SCIENTISTS HAD FOUND ONLY A SINGLE TOOTH, LEAVING THEM UNSURE WHAT KIND OF CREATURE IT WAS UNTIL THEY UNCOVERED MORE FOSSILS.

Maybe that first discovery is why its name means "wounding tooth." More likely, the name comes from the fact that its curved, serrated teeth would have been excellent at biting into prey.

HAVE YOU EVER SEEN A BIRD SITTING ON ITS NEST TO KEEP EGGS WARM? WHEN CREATURES SIT ON THEIR NEST TO HELP EGGS GROW, IT'S CALLED BROODING. FOSSILS FOUND IN MONTANA SHOW EVIDENCE OF NESTS THAT SUGGEST *TROODON* BROODED ITS EGGS.

Troodon may also have lived in small groups, as suggested by discoveries of multiple specimens in the same place.

TROODON MOMS LAID EGGS, BUT PALEONTOLOGISTS HAVE FOUND THAT THE DADS WERE THE ONES WHO SAT ON THE NEST.

Because *Troodon* had forward-facing eyes—giving it binocular vision like we have—paleontologists expect that this dinosaur was a very clever little hunter with the ability to quickly pinpoint scurrying mammals and other small prey.

TROODON HAD A BRAIN THAT WAS MORE THAN FIVE TIMES LARGER THAN EXPECTED FOR A DINOSAUR OF ITS SIZE.

How big do you think dinosaur brains were? Dinosaurs are often ridiculed for having brains "the size of a walnut," but this wasn't true of all species. For its size, *Troodon* actually had a relatively large brain. Paleontologists can tell this from the inside of its skull. Dinosaur brains fit relatively tightly in the bone of the skull, and so the inside of dinosaur skulls preserve what's called a brain endocast. By making molds and 3-D models of this cavity, paleontologists can get a good idea of the size and shape of dinosaur brains.

TELLING HOW SMART *TROODON* WAS IS ANOTHER MATTER, BUT BASED ON WHAT WE KNOW ABOUT ITS LIVING RELATIVES, THIS DINOSAUR MAY HAVE BEEN AS INTELLIGENT AS A RAVEN OR CROW.

Its long, slender limbs suggest that *Troodon* was a fast runner.

SPEED WOULD HAVE BEEN HELPFUL AS BOTH PREDATOR AND PREY. AT JUST 8 FEET (2.4 METERS) AND LESS THAN 100 POUNDS (45 KILOGRAMS), *TROODON* WOULD HAVE BEEN A MIDSIZE DINOSAUR.

GORGOSAURUS LIBRATUS

PRONUNCIATION: GORE-go-SAWR-us

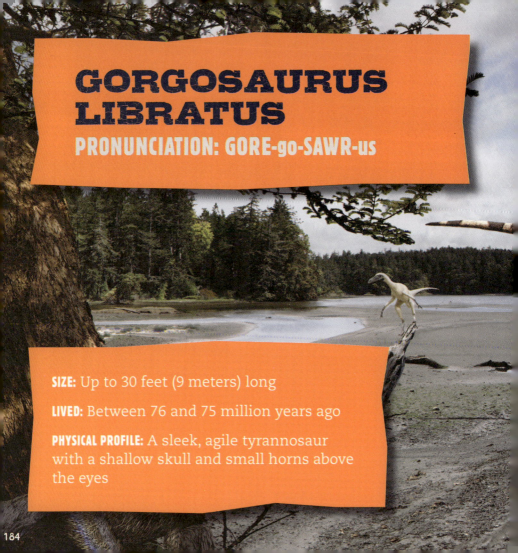

SIZE: Up to 30 feet (9 meters) long

LIVED: Between 76 and 75 million years ago

PHYSICAL PROFILE: A sleek, agile tyrannosaur with a shallow skull and small horns above the eyes

The name *Gorgosaurus* came from the Greek words for "fierce lizard," and this dinosaur was undoubtedly a fearsome creature!

On-screen, you may have seen *Gorgosaurus* in *March of the Dinosaurs* or *Walking with Dinosaurs*.

Gorgosaurus had two fingers that it would have used to catch prey.

As an adult, *Gorgosaurus* could weigh up to 6,000 pounds (2,722 kilograms)!

Gorgosaurus was first described in 1914, and fossils have been found in both the United States and Canada.

Currently, skeletons from over 20 different *Gorgosaurus* have been recovered, which has allowed scientists to study how they changed as they grew.

A YOUNG *GORGOSAURUS* COULD PACK ON THE POUNDS! DURING ITS ADOLESCENCE, *GORGOSAURUS* COULD GAIN OVER 110 POUNDS (50 KILOGRAMS) EACH YEAR!

Prehistoric predators took their meals where they could find them. In many cases, that meant running down dinner. *Gorgosaurus*, for example, had a light build and long legs that made it a very agile hunter, able to outmaneuver some of the herbivorous dinosaurs of its time.

CARNIVORES REGULARLY SCAVENGED, TOO. THANKS TO ITS WELL-DEVELOPED SENSE OF SMELL, *GORGOSAURUS* WAS ABLE TO SNIFF OUT ROTTING CARCASSES AS WELL AS LIVE PREY.

Tyrannosaurids like *Gorgosaurus* were not exclusively hunters or scavengers. They certainly did both to keep up their strength.

LIKE OTHER TYRANNOSAURIDS, *GORGOSAURUS* HAD A LARGE HEAD, SHORT FRONT LIMBS, AND POWERFUL LEGS.

Gorgosaurus was a very close relative of *Albertosaurus sarcophagus* (see page 204), and the two shared a lot of similar features.

IN FACT, SCIENTISTS ORIGINALLY THOUGHT THE TWO MIGHT BE THE SAME SPECIES, AND IT'S STILL DEBATED WHETHER THEY SHOULD ACTUALLY BE CONSIDERED MEMBERS OF THE SAME SPECIES.

Compared to some of the other tyrannosaurids, *Gorgosaurus* was pretty lean, and may have hunted other dinosaurs, although not as heavily armored as those *Daspletosaurus torosus* (see page 192) hunted.

IF YOU'VE EVER WANTED TO BATTLE A DINOSAUR, YOU CAN TAKE ON *GORGOSAURUS* IN VIDEO GAME FORM IN SOME OF THE *JURASSIC WORLD* GAMES.

In reality, not all of these pop culture depictions are accurate. When it was alive, *Gorgosaurus* likely had feathers, a feature that's often left out of digital versions.

LIKE SOME OTHER DINOSAURS, *GORGOSAURUS* WAS NAMED FOR THE GORGONS OF GREEK MYTHOLOGY. IN THE MYTHS, THE GORGONS HAD HAIR MADE OF SNAKES AND COULD TURN THEIR ENEMIES TO STONE.

MAIASAURA PEEBLESORUM

PRONUNCIATION: MY-uh-SORE-a

First discovered in 1978, *Maiasaura* is part of a family of dinosaurs called hadrosaurs that were also known as duck-billed dinosaurs.

SIZE: Up to 30 feet (9 meters) long

LIVED: About 76 million years ago

PHYSICAL PROFILE: *Maiasaura* had a thick tail and a small crest on its head, and because it was a member of the hadrosaurid family, it had a "duck-billed" face with a slightly bill-like snout.

Although many dinosaurs abandoned their young once they hatched, *Maiasaura* often lived alongside its parents for many years and stayed within the herd.

Maiasaura had a small head, squat torso, and thick tail, and it had a very small, almost unnoticeable crest on top of its head.

THESE DINOSAURS TRAVELED IN LARGE HERDS THAT MAY HAVE INCLUDED UP TO A FEW THOUSAND MEMBERS OF DIFFERENT AGES. *MAIASAURA* WERE FAVORED PREY OF DINOSAURS LIKE THE DANGEROUS *TROODON FORMOSUS* (SEE PAGE 180), SO IT WAS SAFER IF THEY TRAVELED IN GROUPS.

Maiasaura earned the name "good mother lizard" because it would lay anywhere from 30 to 40 eggs at a time.

Maiasaura typically walked on all fours, but it may have occasionally stood up on two legs to run away if startled by predators.

Those eggs would have been put in prepared nests called "egg mountains" to incubate.

Unlike dinosaurs like *Oviraptor philoceratops* (see page 176) which could brood its eggs, *Maiasaura* couldn't keep all the eggs warm at once by sitting on the nest, so it likely covered the eggs with vegetation to keep heat in. That vegetation might even have started to rot while the eggs incubated—talk about stinky!

WHY DOESN'T *MAIASAURA* END IN "-SAURUS"? DINOSAUR NAMES ALL COME FROM LATIN, AND IN LATIN THERE ARE MALE AND FEMALE FORMS OF WORDS. MOST DINOSAURS WERE NAMED WITH THE MALE "-SAURUS," BUT BECAUSE *MAIASAURA* WAS THE GOOD MOTHER DINOSAUR, IT WAS GIVEN THE FEMALE "-SAURA" INSTEAD!

TRUE OR FALSE

1. T/F SCIENTISTS HAVE FOUND VERY FEW *LINHERAPTOR EXQUISITUS* FOSSILS.

2. T/F *OVIRAPTOR PHILOCERATOPS* WOULD ABANDON ITS EGGS AFTER THEY WERE LAID.

3. T/F *TROODON FORMOSUS* HAD A BRAIN ABOUT THE SIZE OF A WALNUT.

4. **T/F** WHILE *GORGOSAURUS LIBRATUS* WAS GROWING, IT COULD GAIN OVER 110 POUNDS (50 KILOGRAMS) EVERY YEAR.

5. **T/F** *MAIASAURA PEEBLESORUM* IS ONE OF THE FEW DINOSAURS THAT HAS A FEMALE NAME.

ANSWERS: 1. F; 2. F; 3. F; 4. T; 5. T

DASPLETOSAURUS TOROSUS
PRONUNCIATION: DAS-pleet-uh-SAWR-us

SIZE: Up to 30 feet (9 meters) long and 2.7 tons (2.45 metric tons)

LIVED: 77 to 74 million years ago

PHYSICAL PROFILE: A big, heavily built tyrannosaur with a more powerful bite than its neighbor *Gorgosaurus libratus* (see page 184)

Daspletosaurus would have used its talons to hold down prey while it ate.

Like other tyrannosaurids, *Daspletosaurus* had short arms with two fingers.

With a name like "frightful lizard," it's no doubt that *Daspletosaurus* was a top predator!

Have you ever fought with a sibling? Fights in the tyrannosaur family were often pretty vicious—they went right for the face! Some *Daspletosaurus* skulls have healed bite wounds made by other tyrannosaurs.

DASPLETOSAURUS AND ITS TYRANNOSAUR RELATIVES WERE SOME OF THE LARGEST AND MOST IMPRESSIVE PREDATORS OF THE CRETACEOUS PERIOD.

Daspletosaurus had huge back legs that would have been very powerful. Each foot had three clawed toes, much like talons of modern birds.

SO WHY DID *DASPLETOSAURUS* HAVE SUCH SMALL ARMS? PALEONTOLOGISTS HAVE BEEN PUZZLING OVER THAT MYSTERY SINCE THE FIRST GOOD TYRANNOSAUR SKELETONS WERE DISCOVERED IN THE EARLY TWENTIETH CENTURY. ONE EARLY IDEA WAS THAT TYRANNOSAURS USED THEIR TINY ARMS TO HOLD ONTO THEIR MATES, AND ANOTHER POPULAR GUESS WAS THAT TYRANNOSAURS USED THEIR ARMS TO PUSH THEMSELVES OFF THE GROUND AFTER NAPPING.

Neither idea explains why their arms seem so much smaller than those of their ancestors. That has more to do with the way tyrannosaurs changed their hunting strategy. Small, early tyrannosaurs used their arms to grasp prey, but as tyrannosaurs got larger and started using their jaws to kill and rip apart prey, their skulls evolved to be bigger and carry heavier, stronger muscles.

AS THIS HAPPENED, THEIR ARMS BECAME SMALLER AND SMALLER TO PREVENT THE DINOSAURS FROM BEING FRONT-HEAVY AND FALLING ON THEIR FACES.

This trade-off let tyrannosaurs evolve some of the most powerful jaws of all time, and, although quite small, their arms still had some pretty strong muscles.

WHEN YOU SEE *DASPLETOSAURUS*, CAN YOU PICTURE *TYRANNOSAURUS REX* (SEE PAGE 230)? DUE TO SOME SIMILARITIES, IT'S THOUGHT THAT *DASPLETOSAURUS* MAY HAVE LATER EVOLVED INTO *TYRANNOSAURUS*.

Daspletosaurus would have lived at the same time and in the same habitat as *Albertosaurus sarcophagus* (see page 204) and *Gorgosaurus libratus* (see page 184), which were both relatives.

THOUGH THESE CARNIVORES ALL LIVED IN THE SAME PLACE, THEY MAY HAVE PREYED ON DIFFERENT ANIMALS, LESSENING THE COMPETITION BETWEEN THEM.

Daspletosaurus likely hunted horned dinosaurs called ceratopsians.

DASPLETOSAURUS HAS MADE PLENTY OF ON-SCREEN APPEARANCES, INCLUDING IN BBC'S *PLANET DINOSAUR*.

CARNOTAURUS SASTREI

PRONUNCIATION: CAR-no-TAUR-us

SIZE: About 30 feet (9 meters) long

LIVED: Between 72 and 69 million years ago

PHYSICAL PROFILE: A large carnivore with stubby arms and a deep skull bearing a short, triangular horn projecting over each eye

Fossils of *Carnotaurus* have been found in the Patagonia region of Argentina.

Carnotaurus would have weighed between 4,000 to 6,000 pounds (1,814 to 2,722 kilograms).

Carnotaurus is part of a family of dinosaurs known as Abelisauridae, and members of this family often have odd heads.

A large back part of its jaw indicated that *Carnotaurus* would have had a powerful bite.

Over each eye, *Carnotaurus* had a large brow horn.

Scientist think these horns may have had a purpose in attracting a mate.

CARNOTAURUS HORNS WERE ACTUALLY PART OF THE SKULL BONE, BUT BECAUSE THEY WERE SO SMALL AND BLUNT, THEY LIKELY WEREN'T MUCH USE FOR FIGHTING.

Have you ever seen a bull? They can be pretty intimidating with their long horns. The name *Carnotaurus* means "meat-eating bull." Meat-eating makes sense considering that *Carnotaurus* was a carnivore, and the bull part of its name is a reference to those bull-like horns.

THE HORN BUMPS WEREN'T THE ONLY STRANGE PART OF A *CARNOTAURUS* SKULL. ITS SKULL ALSO HAD A UNIQUE FLAT SHAPE WITH THIN SIDES, WHICH MAY HAVE HELPED *CARNOTAURUS* TO MOVE ITS HEAD QUICKLY. THIS WOULD HAVE BEEN USEFUL FOR RUNNING WHILE IT HUNTED.

Carnotaurus had eyes right at the front of its skull, which would have given it binocular vision.

CARNOTAURUS HAD SOME DANGEROUS TEETH. SCIENTISTS THINK ITS WIDE, BLUNT TEETH COULD HAVE CHOMPED STRAIGHT THROUGH BONE.

The combined force of its teeth and jaws would have made *Carnotaurus* bites especially deadly.

DESPITE ITS HEAVY WEIGHT, *CARNOTAURUS* WAS A PRETTY FAST RUNNER. SCIENTISTS THINK IT COULD REACH UP TO 40 MILES (64 KILOMETERS) PER HOUR. NEXT TIME YOU'RE IN THE CAR YOU CAN LOOK AT THE SPEEDOMETER AND FEEL HOW FAST YOU WOULD NEED TO BE TO OUTRUN *CARNOTAURUS*!

LIKE OTHER CARNIVORES OF THE TIME, *CARNOTAURUS* WOULD HAVE BEEN BIPEDAL, MEANING IT RAN ON TWO LEGS.

Have you ever put your hand up against a window and been able to see all the lines from your hands and fingers in your handprint? Those marks show what your skin looks like. Scientists can look at the marks dinosaur skin left in fossils to learn more about theirs! Impressions found with one specimen indicate that *Carnotaurus* had scaly skin with rows of bigger, flattened bumps.

RELATIVE TO THE SIZE OF ITS BODY, *CARNOTAURUS* HAD VERY SMALL ARMS, EVEN WHEN COMPARED TO OTHER SHORT-ARMED TYRANNOSAURS.

Because of its size, it's likely that those arms were pretty useless.

CARNOTAURUS HAD FOUR FINGERS ON EACH HAND. THREE HAD CLAWS, AND ONLY TWO OF THOSE FINGERS HAD BONES.

Carnotaurus made an on-screen appearance in *Jurassic World*, but the number of claws was different than it would have been in real life. *Carnotaurus* in the movie was also slightly bigger and slower than it would have been in reality.

CARNOTAURUS WAS ALSO FEATURED IN THE DISNEY MOVIE *DINOSAUR*, AND IT WAS ACTUALLY A PRETTY BIG VILLAIN! IN THE MOVIE, A PAIR OF *CARNOTAURUS* HUNTED DOWN THE MAIN CHARACTERS ON THEIR JOURNEY.

There's even a ride version of *Dinosaur* at Disney's Animal Kingdom that includes a menacing *Carnotaurus*.

SAURORNITHOLESTES LANGSTONI

PRONUNCIATION: SAWR-or-NITH-o-LEST-ees

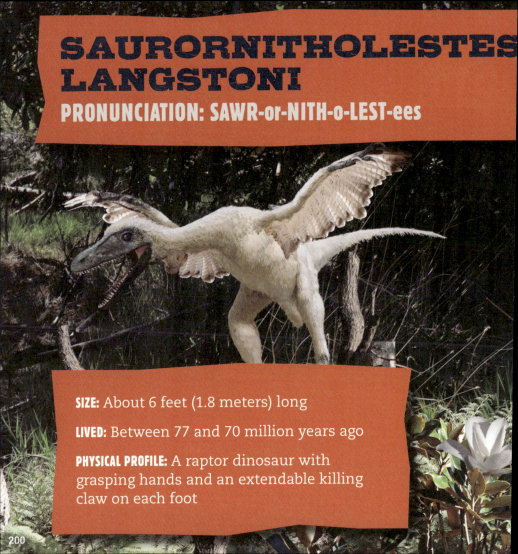

SIZE: About 6 feet (1.8 meters) long

LIVED: Between 77 and 70 million years ago

PHYSICAL PROFILE: A raptor dinosaur with grasping hands and an extendable killing claw on each foot

The skull of *Saurornitholestes* had a large olfactory bulb that scientists think could indicate it had a great sense of smell.

SAURORNITHOLESTES HAD A LONG, CURVED TOE ON EACH FOOT THAT WAS COMMON FOR MEMBERS OF THE DROMAEOSAURIDAE FAMILY, ALSO KNOWN AS RAPTORS.

With large, fanglike teeth, *Saurornitholestes* somewhat resembles its relative *Velociraptor mongoliensis* (see page 118).

LARGE DOESN'T ALWAYS MEAN HEAVY: THOUGH IT WAS ABOUT 6 FEET (1.8 METERS) LONG, SAURORNITHOLESTES WAS FAIRLY LIGHT. IT LIKELY ONLY WEIGHED ABOUT 22 POUNDS (10 KILOGRAMS).

Even predators had to watch out for bigger carnivores. One *Saurornitholestes* jaw shows bite marks from a tyrannosaur that bit the raptor on the face!

SCIENTISTS HAVE DISCOVERED PARTIAL SAURORNITHOLESTES SKELETONS, BUT AS OF YET THEY DON'T HAVE A COMPLETE ONE.

Fossils of *Saurornitholestes* have been found in different parts of the United States and Canada.

MASIAKASAURUS KNOPFLERI

PRONUNCIATION: MA-sheek-ah-SAWR-us

SIZE: About 7 feet (2 meters) long

LIVED: Around 70 million years ago

PHYSICAL PROFILE: A small predator with gnarly, forward-pointed teeth useful for catching fish

Based on the shape of its teeth, it's likely that *Masiakasaurus* ate small animals, but it may have also eaten some fruit.

HOW OLD DO YOU THINK YOU'LL BE WHEN YOU STOP GROWING? FROM STUDIES OF THIS DINOSAUR'S BONE STRUCTURE, PALEONTOLOGISTS HAVE FIGURED OUT THAT IT TOOK ABOUT 10 YEARS FOR *MASIAKASAURUS* TO GROW TO ADULT SIZE.

With the name "vicious lizard," it's easy to see that this dinosaur was a terrific predator.

Fossils of this small, carnivorous theropod have been found in modern-day Madagascar.

Masiakasaurus had forward-projecting, hooked teeth that would have easily latched onto prey.

ALBERTOSAURUS SARCOPHAGUS

PRONUNCIATION: al-BER-tuh-SAWR-us

Albertosaurus had a long tail that would have helped to balance out its heavy head and body.

SIZE: Up to 30 feet (9 meters) long and 1.9 tons (1.7 metric tons)

LIVED: 70 million years ago

PHYSICAL PROFILE: A large, sleek tyrannosaur with a big skull and tiny arms but more agility than the beefier *Tyrannosaurus rex* (see page 230)

Albertosaurus, meaning "lizard from Alberta," was named in 1905, and that's actually the same year that Alberta, Canada, became a province!

The first fossils were found as far back as 1884, and they were some of the first dinosaur remains found in Alberta, Canada.

No one knows exactly why so many died there, but some researchers suspect that it's a clue that *Albertosaurus* lived and hunted in packs.

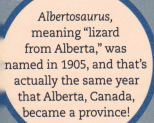

On its hind legs, *Albertosaurus* had four toes, but they weren't all the same size, and one didn't even reach the ground.

In Alberta, Canada, paleontologists have found at least 26 *Albertosaurus* in one place!

ALBERTOSAURUS WAS DISCOVERED BY JOSEPH B. TYRRELL, AGE 25, A GEOLOGIST WHO WAS LOOKING FOR COAL, NOT DINOSAURS!

Although you might picture a predator going after an adult dinosaur, *Albertosaurus* probably targeted easier prey. It could have tried to chomp down on a baby *Spinops sternbergorum* (see page 208) while the infant's parent tried to drive the predator away.

THIS WAS PROBABLY MUCH MORE COMMON THAN ANY SHOWDOWN BETWEEN *ALBERTOSAURUS* AND FULL-GROWN *SPINOPS*.

In a fight, the *Albertosaurus* would be much more likely to suffer injuries that could harm its ability to hunt. Infant dinosaurs, as well as those too old or sick to defend themselves, were much safer targets.

IN FACT, THIS MAY BE WHY INFANT DINOSAURS ARE SO RARE IN THE FOSSIL RECORD AND WHY YOUNG DINOSAURS GREW QUICKLY. PREDATORS OFTEN PICKED OFF BABY AND JUVENILE DINOSAURS, AND ONE OF THE FEW WAYS TO AVOID BECOMING A SNACK WAS TO GROW UP FAST.

ALTHOUGH MASSIVE COMPARED TO OTHER DINOSAURS, ALBERTOSAURUS WAS SMALLER THAN MANY OF ITS RELATIVES IN THE TYRANNOSAUR FAMILY.

Like the other tyrannosaurids, *Albertosaurus* was a bipedal dinosaur with a heavy body, large head, short arms, and two fingers.

TWO FOSSILS OF ALBERTOSAURUS SHOW SKIN IMPRESSIONS THAT TELL SCIENTISTS ALBERTOSAURUS HAD SCALES ON ITS SKIN.

Albertosaurus had long, sawlike teeth that were great at tearing flesh, but not so great at chewing food. It's likely that it swallowed large chunks whole.

ALBERTOSAURUS SPECIMENS THAT HAVE BEEN FOUND HAVE A WIDE AGE RANGE FROM 2 YEARS OLD TO 20 YEARS OLD, WHICH GIVES SCIENTISTS THE CHANCE TO STUDY HOW THIS DINOSAUR GREW.

Albertosaurus actually had horns over its eyes, and scientists think they may have even been colored. They were likely used to identify other *Albertosaurus* or for mating.

SPINOPS STERNBERGORUM

PRONUNCIATION: Spy-nops

SIZE: About 23 feet (7 meters) long

LIVED: 70 million years ago

PHYSICAL PROFILE: A large herbivore with a nose horn, bony neck frill, and two large horns over its eyes

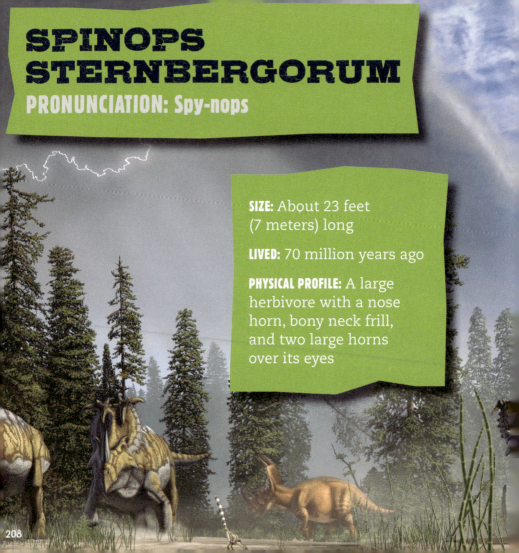

Although the first *Spinops* fossils were found in 1916 in Alberta, Canada, scientists didn't describe the species until nearly a century later.

THE FOSSILS WERE SENT TO THE NATURAL HISTORY MUSEUM IN LONDON, WHERE THE CURATORS DIDN'T THINK THEY WERE WORTHWHILE, AND THEY WERE PUT IN STORAGE AND FORGOTTEN ABOUT. IF YOU'VE EVER LOST SOMETHING IN YOUR ROOM FOR A WHILE, YOU'LL UNDERSTAND.

In 2011, the fossils were rediscovered and examined.

ONCE SCIENTISTS REALIZED WHAT THE FOSSILS WERE, THE SPECIMENS WERE DECLARED TO BE A NEW SPECIES AND WERE APPROPRIATELY GIVEN A NAME THAT MEANS "SPINED FACE."

SCIENTISTS NOW HAVE TWO PARTIAL SKULLS OF *SPINOPS* TO EXAMINE.

Spinops skulls show the presence of three horns, two over the eyes and one on the nose.

SCIENTISTS CAN ALSO TELL THAT *SPINOPS* HAD A PROMINENT NECK FRILL, BECAUSE PORTIONS OF IT WERE PRESERVED IN THE FOSSILS.

Because they haven't found many fossils yet, scientists don't know much about *Spinops*. Unless, of course, more fossils are hiding in other museum storerooms!

DINO QUIZ

1. WHICH DINOSAUR MAY HAVE LATER EVOLVED INTO *TYRANNOSAURUS REX*?

A. *DASPLETOSAURUS TOROSUS*

B. *SAURORNITHOLESTES LANGSTONI*

C. *MASIAKASAURUS KNOPFLERI*

D. *SPINOPS STERNBERGORUM*

2. HOW FAST COULD THE "MEAT-EATING BULL" *CARNOTAURUS SASTREI* RUN TO CATCH ITS PREY?

A. 10 MILES (16 KILOMETERS) PER HOUR

B. 20 MILES (32 KILOMETERS) PER HOUR

C. 30 MILES (48 KILOMETERS) PER HOUR

D. 40 MILES (64 KILOMETERS) PER HOUR

3. **WHICH CREATURE SOMEWHAT RESEMBLES ITS RELATIVE VELOCIRAPTOR MONGOLIENSIS?**

A. *MASIAKASAURUS KNOPFLERI*

B. *ALBERTOSAURUS SARCOPHAGUS*

C. *CARNOTAURUS SASTREI*

D. *SAURORNITHOLESTES LANGSTONI*

4. **WHERE HAVE *ALBERTOSAURUS SARCOPHAGUS* FOSSILS BEEN FOUND?**

A. NORTH AMERICA

B. SOUTH AMERICA

C. AFRICA

D. ASIA

5. **WHICH DINOSAUR FOSSILS SAT IN A MUSEUM STOREROOM FOR ALMOST 100 YEARS BEFORE SCIENTISTS REALIZED WHAT THEY WERE?**

A. *ALBERTOSAURUS SARCOPHAGUS*

B. *DASPLETOSAURUS TOROSUS*

C. *SPINOPS STERNBERGORUM*

D. *SAURORNITHOLESTES LANGSTONI*

Answers: 1. A; 2. C; 3. D; 4. A; 5. C

ORNITHOMIMUS EDMONTICUS

PRONUNCIATION: OR-nith-o-MIME-us

SIZE: About 12 feet (3.6 meters) long

LIVED: Around 70 million years ago

PHYSICAL PROFILE: An ostrich-mimic dinosaur with long arms, graceful neck, and a toothless beak suited to eating plants as well as insects and small prey

Fossils of *Ornithomimus* have been found all across North America in both Canada and the United States.

Adult *Ornithomimus* looked different than its babies. It had long feathers growing from its arms, somewhat similar to the plumes on the arms of ostriches today.

Ornithomimus is called an "ostrich mimic" because it shares a lot of similarities with modern-day ostriches.

Ornithomimus was toothless, but it could have used its long arms and large claws to snatch small prey as well as pull down tree branches.

IT MAY HAVE ALSO USED ITS CLAWS TO DIG IN THE DIRT, AND IT WAS LIKELY AN OMNIVOROUS CREATURE.

Baby dinosaurs weren't tiny copies of their parents. Dinosaurs changed dramatically as they grew up—kind of like us—and that's true of their body coverings as well as their bones. Thanks to recent discoveries in Canada, paleontologists now know that baby *Ornithomimus* were covered with a coating of chick-like fuzz.

THIS FUZZ PROBABLY KEPT THE LITTLE ONES WARM AND, DEPENDING ON THE COLORS, COULD HAVE PROVIDED THEM CAMOUFLAGE TO HIDE FROM THE LIKES OF ALBERTOSAURUS SARCOPHAGUS (SEE PAGE 204).

Maybe this Cretaceous dinosaur used its arm feathers like its modern cousins, flailing them around in mating displays and covering its nests to keep its eggs warm.

ORNITHOMIMUS HAD LEGS THAT WERE MADE FOR RUNNING, AND IT WAS EASILY ONE OF THE FASTEST CREATURES AROUND.

Ornithomimus could reach somewhere between 35 and 40 miles (56 to 64 kilometers) per hour, which would have helped it to escape predators. A modern ostrich can run at about the same speed!

ORNITHOMIMUS HAD A FEATHERED TAIL THAT MAY HAVE HELPED IT TO MANEUVER WHILE IT RAN.

One fossil found actually had preserved tail feathers, which helped scientists to understand that this dinosaur had plumage on its tail, but the lower part of its legs didn't have feathers.

BY COMPARING IT TO A MODERN OSTRICH, WHICH ALSO HAS SOME AREAS OF BARE SKIN, SCIENTISTS CAN SPECULATE THAT ORNITHOMIMUS MAY HAD FEATHERS IN SOME SPOTS TO HELP REGULATE ITS TEMPERATURE.

THERIZINOSAURUS CHELONIFORMIS

PRONUNCIATION: THER-ih-ZEE-no-SAWR-us

The first *Therizinosaurus* fossils were found in Mongolia in 1948, but it was originally misidentified as a prehistoric turtle.

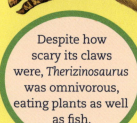

Despite how scary its claws were, *Therizinosaurus* was omnivorous, eating plants as well as fish.

SIZE: About 33 feet (10 meters) long

LIVED: 70 million years ago

PHYSICAL PROFILE: A large, tubby dinosaur with a tiny head, long neck, and 10-foot (3-meter)-long arms tipped with 3-foot (1-meter)-long claws at the end

Have you ever seen a cartoon of the grim reaper? Usually, he's shown walking around with a big, curved blade called a scythe. *Therizinosaurus* means "scythe lizard," and the name is undoubtedly a reference to the shape of this dinosaur's huge, curved claws.

As more fossils were discovered, it was clear that this creature, which could grow to be at least 1,000 pounds (454 kilograms), was actually a dinosaur, not a turtle!

In fact, those claws were long, but not particularly sharp, which could have indicated that they were used to gather leaves into its mouth or to dig into mounds of termites.

Therizinosaurus had a small head and neck compared to its large, squat body.

Its four-toed feet likely didn't move very quickly, so it's doubtful that *Therizinosaurus* was a fast runner.

QUETZALCOATLUS NORTHROPI

PRONUNCIATION: KWET-zal-koh-AT-lus

SIZE: A wingspan of up to 36 feet (11 meters) and a height as tall as a giraffe

LIVED: 68 million years ago

PHYSICAL PROFILE: One of the biggest flying animals ever, with wings made up of skin stretched between the body and extremely long fourth fingers

Quetzalcoatlus hunted much like storks do today, stalking small prey—like baby dinosaurs—and plucking them up with its toothless beak.

An intimidating presence, *Quetzalcoatlus* could stand as tall as a giraffe and spread its wings more than 30 feet (9 meters) wide.

"QUETZALCOATLUS" MIGHT SOUND LIKE A MOUTHFUL, BUT IT ACTUALLY REFERS TO THE MESOAMERICAN GOD QUETZALCOATL, WHO WAS ALSO SOMETIMES KNOWN AS A "FEATHERED SERPENT." THE GOD WAS KNOWN FOR BEING FEARSOME AND POWERFUL AND FOR BEING ABLE TO CONTROL THE WIND. THIS CERTAINLY SOUNDS LIKE A GOOD NAME FOR A FLYING PREDATOR!

Have you ever seen an image of a stork dropping off a baby? You might think those birds are just fiction, but there are actually real birds and they're not as friendly as their cartoon counterparts. In fact, they're actually hunters! Though *Quetzalcoatlus* was a feathered reptile, not a bird, it had a body that was similar to a bat and a head that was similar to a stork (but much larger, of course).

PTEROSAURS LIKE *QUETZALCOATLUS* WEREN'T ABLE TO FLAP THEIR WINGS MUCH BECAUSE OF THEIR HUGE SIZE, SO IT'S LIKELY THAT THEY RELIED ON GLIDING TO GET AROUND. IN FACT, SOME PREHISTORIC TRACKS REVEAL THAT QUETZALCOATLUS DID SOMETIMES WALK.

Unfortunately for scientists, they don't have a *Quetzalcoatlus* skeleton that's anywhere near complete, so it's difficult to understand how exactly this massive creature was able to fly.

QUETZALCOATLUS WOULD HAVE BEEN ABLE TO TRAVEL LONG DISTANCES, AND SOME SCIENTISTS THINK THAT IT MAY HAVE BEEN ABLE TO TRAVEL 10,000 MILES (16,093 METERS) AT A TIME. THE DISTANCE FROM THE EAST COAST OF THE UNITED STATES TO THE WEST COAST IS JUST UNDER 3,000 MILES (4,828 KILOMETERS). THAT MEANS THAT *QUETZALCOATLUS* COULD FLY FROM ONE SIDE OF THE COUNTRY TO THE OTHER THREE TIMES WITHOUT TAKING A BREAK!

To make the trip, Quetzalcoatlus would have needed to stay in the air for more than a week!

SO IF MOST PLANES NEED A BREAK DURING TRIPS THAT LONG, HOW DID *QUETZALCOATLUS* MANAGE IT? TO DO THIS, *QUETZALCOATLUS* WOULD HAVE NEEDED TO USE COLUMNS OF HOT AIR AND AN OCCASIONAL WING FLAP TO KEEP IT IN FLIGHT, AND IT WOULD HAVE TRAVELED AT AROUND 80 MILES (129 KILOMETERS) PER HOUR.

Just because this predator was comfortable in the air, doesn't mean it wouldn't have been terrifying on land. *Quetzalcoatlus* had long legs and would have been able to walk as well.

HOW BIG WAS

20 FEET TALL (6 METERS)

Quetzalcoatlus northropi

30 FEET (9 METERS) WIDE WINGSPAN

QUETZALCOATLUS NORTHROPI?

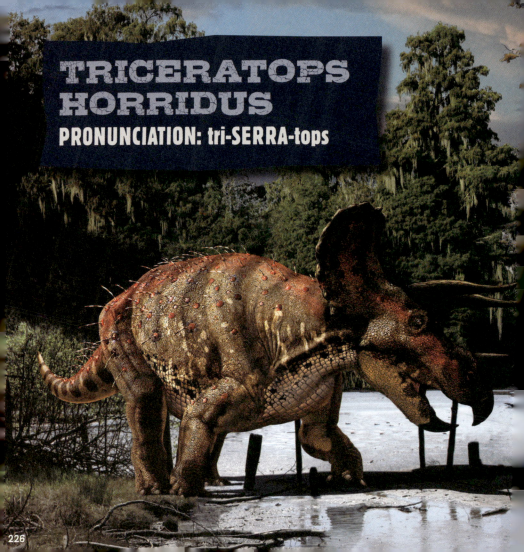

TRICERATOPS HORRIDUS
PRONUNCIATION: tri-SERRA-tops

SIZE: About 29 feet (8.8 meters) long

LIVED: 68 to 66 million years ago

PHYSICAL PROFILE: A large herbivore with three horns on its face

WHEN YOU PICTURE A DINOSAUR, YOUR FIRST THOUGHT MIGHT BE *TRICERATOPS*. IT'S EASILY ONE OF THE MOST RECOGNIZABLE AND MOST POPULAR DINOSAURS WITH ITS THREE SKULL HORNS AND BONY NECK FRILL.

Its name might seem obvious, but *Triceratops* means "three-horned face."

HAVE YOU EVER WANTED TO GO BACK IN TIME TO MEET A DINOSAUR? IF YOU WERE TRAVELING BACK, *TRICERATOPS* MIGHT BE ONE OF THE FIRST YOU'D FIND! THOUGH *TRICERATOPS* WAS ABSOLUTELY ANCIENT, IT WAS ACTUALLY ONE OF THE MOST RECENT DINOSAURS, LIKELY BECOMING EXTINCT DURING A MASS EXTINCTION ABOUT 65 MILLION YEARS AGO.

NUMEROUS *TRICERATOPS* REMAINS HAVE BEEN FOUND THROUGHOUT NORTH AMERICA SINCE *TRICERATOPS* WAS FIRST DISCOVERED IN 1889.

Does *Triceratops* look like it could exist today? *Triceratops* is actually somewhat similar to a modern rhinoceros, and it carried its heavy body on four legs.

The terrifying *Tyrannosaurus rex* (see page 230) would have hunted *Triceratops*. In fact, one *Triceratops* fossil found in 1997 had a horn that was bitten off, and the bite marks matched the teeth of *Tyrannosaurus*.

THAT PARTICULAR *TRICERATOPS* WAS LUCKY ENOUGH TO ESCAPE BEING EATEN BY *TYRANNOSAURUS*. THE HORN SHOWED SIGNS OF HEALING, MEANING THAT WASN'T WHAT CAUSED ITS DEATH.

Some *Triceratops* fossils showed punctures on the neck frills that were caused by other *Triceratops*, which tells scientists they may have fought each other using their horns. It's likely that these battles were over a mate.

ALTHOUGH SOME HORNED DINOSAUR FOSSILS HAVE BEEN FOUND GROUPED TOGETHER AS IF THEY TRAVELED IN HERDS, MOST *TRICERATOPS* FOSSILS WERE DISCOVERED ALONE.

Scientists actually debate what exactly the purpose of the horns and neck frills would have been. It's likely that they were used for protection, but there could have been other reasons for their presence.

TYRANNOSAURUS REX

PRONUNCIATION: tye-RAN-uh-SAWR-us

Tyrannosaurus would have reached full size by age 20, but even before it had finished growing, this massive creature was a formidable predator.

SIZE: Up to 40 feet (15 meters) long and 9 tons (8 metric tons)

LIVED: 68 to 66 million years ago

PHYSICAL PROFILE: A gigantic carnivore with a large, deep skull and comparatively tiny, two-fingered arms

Fossils have been located in the Northwest of the United States as well as in Alberta, Canada.

The oldest *Tyrannosaurus* fossil analyzed was over 30 years old when it died.

Although this species is one of the most well known to the public, scientists actually don't have a complete skeleton of this massive dinosaur.

Tyrannosaurus rex truly was the king in the age of dinosaurs.

In fact, its name actually loosely translates from Latin to "king of the tyrant lizards."

The first *Tyrannosaurus* fossil to be discovered was located by the curator of the American Museum of Natural History, and the museum in New York City is one of the few places you can see a true *Tyrannosaurus* fossil on display.

IF YOU'VE EVER PICTURED *TYRANNOSAURUS* VICIOUSLY SNAPPING, YOU'D BE EXACTLY RIGHT. *TYRANNOSAURUS* COULD RAM ITS SERRATED, RAIL SPIKE-SIZED TEETH INTO PREY WITH A FORCE OF MORE THAN 12,800 POUNDS (5,806 KILOGRAMS), EASILY PUNCTURING FLESH AND BONE.

This let *Tyrannosaurus* take down its victims as well as thoroughly consume carcasses, and, from fossilized *Tyrannosaurus* dung (called coprolites) with bone and muscle inside, we know it really did swallow giant mouthfuls of flesh.

ITS JAW MUSCLES WERE JUST PART OF WHAT MADE *TYRANNOSAURUS* SO UNBEATABLE. THE NECK MUSCLES OF *TYRANNOSAURUS* WERE EXCEPTIONALLY STRONG.

Those strong muscles allowed *Tyrannosaurus* to kill prey with a side-to-side shake of its head, and, as paleontologists know from bitten bones, their powerful jaws could easily injure even horned dinosaurs like *Triceratops horridus* (see page 226).

MORE THAN THAT, PALEONTOLOGISTS HAVE CALCULATED THAT *TYRANNOSAURUS* HAD NECK MUSCLES STRONG ENOUGH TO THROW A 110-POUND (50-KILOGRAM) CHUNK OF MEAT 15 FEET (4.5 METERS) INTO THE AIR AND CATCH IT AGAIN. TO *TYRANNOSAURUS*, YOU'D BE JUST A QUICK BITE.

In the movie *Jurassic Park*, a *Tyrannosaurus* is shown biting the roof of a car right off. This wasn't an exaggeration. Based on its strength, this would have been entirely possible for *Tyrannosaurus*!

THE CARNIVOROUS *TYRANNOSAURUS* WOULD HAVE BEEN A THREAT TO JUST ABOUT ANY DINOSAUR IT ENCOUNTERED.

Tyrannosaurus wouldn't pass up a free meal, even a member of its own species. Some *Tyrannosaurus* skeletons show bite marks that could only have been caused by other *Tyrannosaurus*.

SCIENTISTS USED THE DISTANCE BETWEEN FOSSIL TRACKS TO GUESS AT HOW FAST *TYRANNOSAURUS* COULD MOVE. ALTHOUGH IT'S HIGHLY DEBATABLE, IT LIKELY WALKED AT ABOUT 3 TO 6 MILES (4.8 TO 9.6 KILOMETERS) PER HOUR AND COULD ONLY RUN ABOUT 10 MILES (16 KILOMETERS) PER HOUR.

That may not seem very fast (and compared to other smaller dinosaurs it's certainly not very speedy), but *Tyrannosaurus* relied on its size and power, not its speed, to catch prey.

AT THE TOP OF ITS HEAD, *TYRANNOSAURUS* HAD TWO HOLES THAT SCIENTISTS DIDN'T UNDERSTAND. AS RECENTLY AS SEPTEMBER 2019, SCIENTISTS WERE DEBATING THE PURPOSE OF THE HOLES, BUT THE NEWEST RESEARCH SUGGESTS THAT THEY MAY HAVE HELPED TO REGULATE TEMPERATURE.

Tyrannosaurus walked on two legs, but it likely didn't stand fully upright. As it walked, it would have been tilted forward to be somewhat parallel to the ground.

ITS MASSIVE TAIL WOULD HAVE COUNTERBALANCED THE WEIGHT OF ITS HEAD AS IT MOVED.

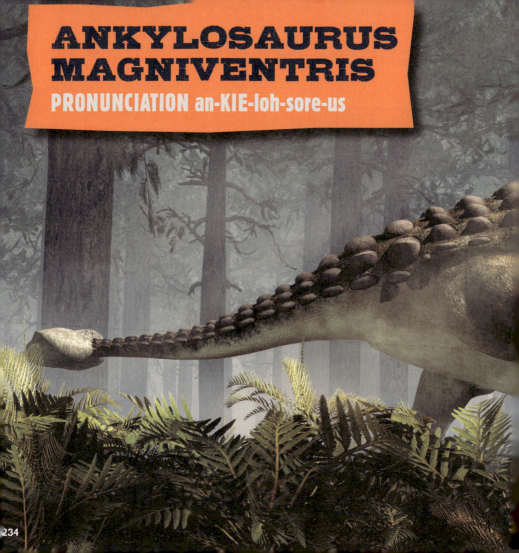

ANKYLOSAURUS MAGNIVENTRIS

PRONUNCIATION an-KIE-loh-sore-us

SIZE: About 20 feet (6 meters) long

LIVED: 66 to 65 million years ago

PHYSICAL PROFILE: This armored dinosaur was covered in thick bone plates and had a clublike tail.

IF YOU CAN PICTURE AN ARMY TANK, IT MIGHT HELP YOU TO BETTER UNDERSTAND HOW ANKYLOSAURUS WAS BUILT.

The most impressive part of *Ankylosaurus* is its "armor" made of thick bone plates called osteoderms or scutes.

THESE TYPES OF BONE PLATES ARE SIMILAR TO WHAT YOU MIGHT SEE ON A MODERN CROCODILE OR ARMADILLO, AND THEY HELPED TO PROTECT *ANKYLOSAURUS* FROM DANGEROUS PREDATORS.

Those plates weren't the only thing protecting *Ankylosaurus*. On its head, *Ankylosaurus* had two horns that pointed back and down.

FOSSILS OF *ANKYLOSAURUS* HAVE BEEN FOUND IN WESTERN NORTH AMERICA, BUT A FULL SKELETON HAS NOT YET BEEN DISCOVERED.

With small, leaf-shaped teeth, *Ankylosaurus* was likely an herbivore.

THE SHAPE OF ITS TAIL WAS CLUBLIKE, WHICH MAY HAVE ALLOWED *ANKYLOSAURUS* TO USE IT AS A WEAPON.

Have you ever worn a helmet when you ride a bike? *Ankylosaurus* had a wide, heavily armored skull to protect its head, much like a helmet.

THE NAME *ANKYLOSAURUS* MEANS "FUSED LIZARD," PARTS OF THIS DINOSAUR'S BODY AND SKULL WERE FUSED TOGETHER

TRUE OR FALSE

1. T / F *ORNITHOMIMUS EDMONTICUS HAD A BODY SHAPE THAT'S SIMILAR TO MODERN-DAY OSTRICHES.*

2. T / F *QUETZALCOATLUS NORTHROPI WASN'T A VERY GOOD FLIER AND COULD ONLY GLIDE DOWN FROM TREES.*

3. T / F *TRICERATOPS HORRIDUS WERE SOMETIMES UNLUCKY PREY FOR TYRANNOSAURUS REX.*

4. T/F TYRANNOSAURUS REX WAS ONE OF THE FASTEST PREDATORS IN THE CRETACEOUS PERIOD.

5. T/F ANKYLOSAURUS MAGNIVENTRIS WAS COVERED IN BONY "ARMOR" THAT IT USED FOR DEFENSE.

ANSWERS: 1. T; 2. F; 3. T; 4. F; 5. T

CENOZOIC ERA

66 MILLION YEARS AGO TO PRESENT

The name "Cenozoic" means "new life," and it was certainly a time for new beginnings in the animal kingdom. After the reigning dinosaurs were wiped out at the end of the Cretaceous period, it was time for a new group of animals to take over as the dominant creatures. The climate was continuing to warm, and habitats and plants were changing along with it. Species were starting to diversify even more, and mammals in particular were growing larger and stronger and conquering both land and sea, paving the way for them (and later for humans) to take over as top of the food chain.

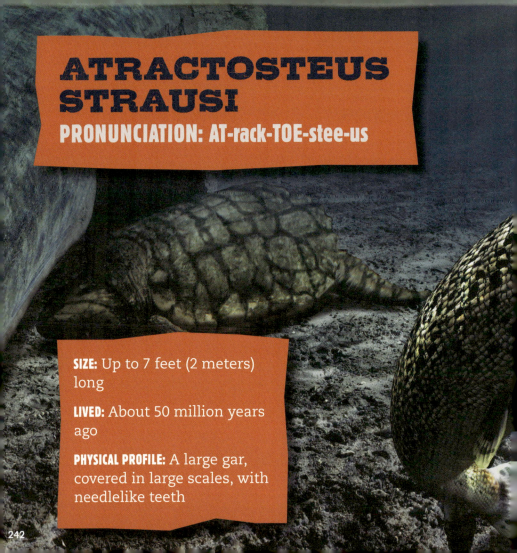

ATRACTOSTEUS STRAUSI

PRONUNCIATION: AT-rack-TOE-stee-us

SIZE: Up to 7 feet (2 meters) long

LIVED: About 50 million years ago

PHYSICAL PROFILE: A large gar, covered in large scales, with needlelike teeth

PALEONTOLOGISTS KNOW A GREAT DEAL ABOUT WHAT *ATRACTOSTEUS* LOOKED LIKE BECAUSE PREHISTORIC LAKES CONTAINED EXQUISITELY PRESERVED FOSSILS THAT INCLUDE THE SCALES IN PLACE.

Atractosteus was part of an alligator-like family of creatures called gar.

THE NAME *ATRACTOSTEUS* COMES FROM THE GREEK WORD *ATRACTOS*, WHICH MEANS "ARROW."

YOU MIGHT KNOW THAT FISH HAVE GILLS, BUT HAVE YOU EVER WONDERED HOW OTHER UNDERWATER CREATURES ARE ABLE TO BREATHE? GAR HAVE SPECIAL ORGANS CALLED "SWIM BLADDERS" THAT FUNCTION LIKE LUNGS.

Do you like seafood? *Atractosteus* likely ate fish and some crustaceans.

ALTHOUGH THEY WERE SLOW-MOVING AT TIMES, THESE CARNIVORES COULD MOVE QUICKLY WHEN THEY WERE ON THE HUNT FOR PREY.

EOHIPPUS ANGUSTIDENS

PRONUNCIATION: EE-oh-HIP-us

SIZE: About 2 feet (0.6 meters) high

LIVED: About 55 to 45 million years ago

PHYSICAL PROFILE: This mammal had a deerlike body with a horselike head.

Eohippus had slender legs that would have been useful for outrunning predators because this herbivore would likely have been a target for vicious carnivores.

Though it looks more like a deer, *Eohippus* is actually considered one of the first horses to have walked Earth.

In fact, its name actually means "dawn horse," a reference to its place as the first in the line of horses.

Though sometimes depicted as smaller, *Eohippus* was about 2 feet (0.6 meter) high and weighed around 50 pounds (23 kilograms)—about the same size as a border collie!

Interestingly, *Eohippus* had different numbers of toes on its feet. The front two feet had four toes, but the back two feet just had three toes.

Based on its teeth shape, scientists think *Eohippus* probably ate low-hanging leaves, not grass like modern horses.

DORUDON ATROX

PRONUNCIATION: DORR-oo-DON

SIZE: About 16 feet (4.8 meters) long

LIVED: 40.4 to 33.9 million years ago

PHYSICAL PROFILE: An early whale with pointed, grabbing teeth at the front of the jaw and shearing teeth in the cheek

Can you picture a whale that could walk on land? It might sound ridiculous, but about 55 million years ago, the land-based ancestors of whales started to walk into the ocean. They started out as hoofed mammals that swam in the lakes and rivers, and, in time, their generations became increasingly adapted to life in the water. By about 40 million years ago, the walking whales had given rise to ones that lived entirely at sea, like *Dorudon*.

IF IT LIVED IN THE WATER, WHY DID IT HAVE LEGS? *DORUDON* WAS PART OF THE EVOLUTIONARY PROCESS FROM WALKING TO SWIMMING. THE SMALL, FINLIKE LEGS STICKING OUT FROM THE SIDES OF *DORUDON* CONNECT BACK TO ITS AMPHIBIOUS ANCESTORS, BUT ITS LEGS LIKELY WEREN'T VERY USEFUL FOR WALKING OR MOVING ON LAND.

What's the last thing you ate? *Dorudon* was a ferocious sea predator, and scientists have actually found fossilized stomach contents showing that the last thing this prehistoric whale fed on was fish.

THE NAME *DORUDON* MEANS "SPEAR-TOOTH," AND THIS SEA CREATURE DID IN FACT HAVE A MOUTHFUL OF SPEARLIKE TEETH.

Adult *Dorudon* were pretty big creatures, but baby *Dorudon* had to watch out for bigger whales. Bite marks on one young *Dorudon* skull show it was killed by something bigger, possibly another early whale named *Basilosaurus* isis.

DORUDON WOULD HAVE HAD A LONG, NARROW SNOUT. MODERN BEAKED WHALES HAVE A SIMILAR SNOUT SHAPE, BUT DORUDON WOULDN'T HAVE HAD A LARGE "MELON." MODERN WHALES HAVE A BULGING AREA OF THEIR HEAD CALLED A MELON THAT'S OFTEN IMPORTANT FOR ECHOLOCATION.

Did you know that there were once prehistoric seas that no longer exist? *Dorudon* fossils come from an area in Egypt called the Tethys Sea, which was an ancient body of water that used to connect the Mediterranean Sea and the Indian Ocean but is now land. This area is known as the "Valley of the Whales," because fossils from whale ancestors have been found there.

LIKE MODERN WHALES, DORUDON HAD A VERY LARGE HOLE IN ITS LOWER JAW THAT MAY HAVE BEEN USEFUL FOR HEARING UNDERWATER.

Because of its teeth and jaw shape, scientists speculate that *Dorudon* may have also eaten some small marine mammals.

CARCHAROCLES MEGALODON

PRONUNCIATION: CAR-CHAR-oh-clays

SIZE: Up to 52 feet (15.8 meters) long and 65 tons (59 metric tons)

LIVED: 28 to 4 million years ago

PHYSICAL PROFILE: The largest shark of all time, similar in form to today's great whites but with more finely serrated teeth

Of all the sharks to ever swim the seas, *Carcharocles* was the biggest.

MEGALODON MEANS "GIANT TOOTH," AND IT'S NO SURPRISE WHY. THIS CREATURE'S SERRATED TEETH HAD A TRIANGULAR SHAPE SIMILAR TO A MODERN WHITE SHARK.

Though they were similar shapes, a white shark's tooth is usually about 2 inches (5 centimeters) long, whereas *Carcharocles* had teeth that were nearly 7 inches (17.8 centimeters) long!

FROM TOOTH MARKS ON BONES, PALEONTOLOGISTS KNOW THAT *CARCHAROCLES MEGALODON* FREQUENTLY FED ON BLUBBERY WHALES.

We don't have to worry about any of these giants showing up at the beach today, though. The fossil record shows that this enormous shark went extinct about two million years ago, long before humans started hitting the beach.

CARCHAROCLES ROAMED THE SEAS FOR MILLIONS OF YEARS—NEARLY 14 MILLION YEARS TO BE EXACT! CARCHAROCLES FOSSILS HAVE BEEN FOUND ON EVERY CONTINENT EXCEPT ANTARCTICA, SHOWING THAT THERE WAS LITTLE OCEAN WHERE THIS CREATURE WOULDN'T VENTURE.

Scientists think that *Carcharocles* may have preferred warmer waters, but had a specialized way of regulating its temperature that's similar to white sharks, which are not exclusively warm-blooded. This would have allowed them to swim in colder water that other predators didn't access, putting them at the top of the food chain.

EVEN BABY *CARCHAROCLES* WERE MASSIVE. SCIENTISTS ESTIMATED THE SIZE OF JUVENILE *CARCHAROCLES* BASED ON THEIR TEETH AND THINK THAT THEY MAY HAVE BEEN ABOUT 6.5 FEET (2 METERS) AT BIRTH.

Human babies sometimes stay in nurseries, but have you ever heard of an animal nursery? Scientists think that young *Carcharocles* may have lived in "nurseries" in shallow water where older *Carcharocles* could protect them from attacks. When they were fully grown, they would have left the nursery alone to find deeper water and hunt for prey.

CARCHAROCLES WOULD NEVER HAVE ENCOUNTERED A DINOSAUR. IT LIVED MORE THAN 40 MILLION YEARS AFTER DINOSAURS BECAME EXTINCT.

DINO QUIZ

1. **WHAT DID ATRACTOSTEUS STRAUSI EAT?**

    A. FISH

    B. BIRDS

    C. REPTILES

    D. PLANTS

2. **WHICH MODERN ANIMAL IS ABOUT THE SAME SIZE AS *EOHIPPUS ANGUSTIDENS*?**

    A. MOUSE

    B. DOG

    C. HORSE

    D. ELEPHANT

3. WHICH OF THESE CREATURES IS RELATED TO MODERN WHALES?

A. CARCHAROCLES MEGALODON

B. DORUDON ATROX

C. EOHIPPUS ANGUSTIDENS

D. ATRACTOSTEUS STRAUSI

4. HOW BIG WERE *CARCHAROCLES MEGALODON* TEETH?

A. 3 INCHES (7.6 CENTIMETERS)

B. 5 INCHES (12.7 CENTIMETERS)

C. 7 INCHES (17.8 CENTIMETERS)

D. 9 INCHES (22.8 CENTIMETERS)

5. WHICH CREATURE RAISED ITS YOUNG IN "NURSERIES"?

A. CARCHAROCLES MEGALODON

B. DORUDON ATROX

C. EOHIPPUS ANGUSTIDENS

D. ATRACTOSTEUS STRAUSI

Answers: 1. A; 2. B; 3. B; 4. C; 5. A

HYAENODON GIGAS
PRONUNCIATION: HIGH-ay-NO-don

SIZE: 10 feet (3 meters) long and up to 1,100 pounds (500 kilograms)

LIVED: 42 to 15.9 million years ago

PHYSICAL PROFILE: A four-legged mammal with piercing teeth at the front of the jaw and cheek teeth that slid past each other to maintain a sharp cutting edge

DINICTIS FELINA
PRONUNCIATION: DY-nick-TIS

SIZE: Almost 4 feet (1.2 meters) long

LIVED: 37.2 to 20.4 million years ago

PHYSICAL PROFILE: A catlike "false saber-tooth" with retractable claws and elongated canines

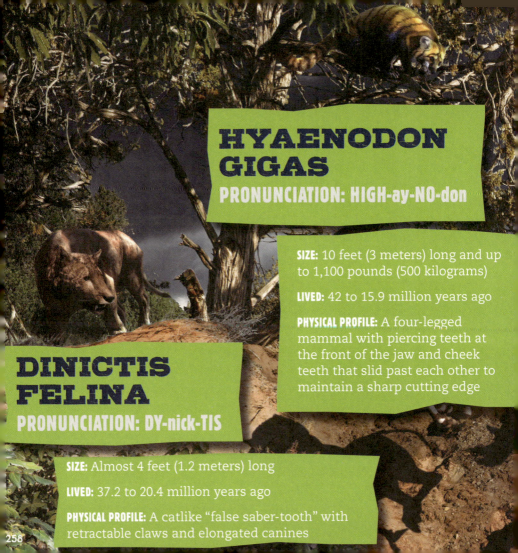

ARCHAEOTHERIUM MORTONI

PRONUNCIATION: AR-kay-o-THEER-ee-um

SIZE: About 7 feet (2 meters) long

LIVED: 38 to 24.8 million years ago

PHYSICAL PROFILE: A piglike hoofed mammal with long jaws fitted with piercing, slicing, and crushing teeth

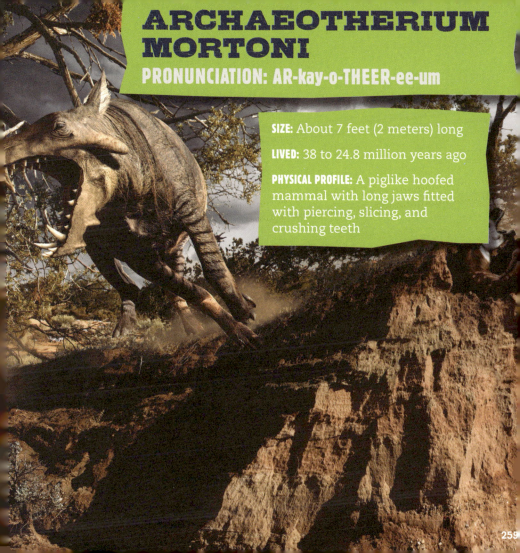

DINICTIS FELINA

THE NAME *DINICTIS* ACTUALLY MEANS "TERRIBLE CAT," WHICH GIVES US A GOOD CLUE AS TO WHAT THIS PREDATOR LOOKED LIKE AND HOW VICIOUS IT WAS.

Have you ever seen a lion or a tiger? Those big cats are hunters and are a lot different from normal house cats, but all modern cats big and small can be tied back to ancestors that lived a few million years ago. Although it looked and hunted like a cat, *Dinictis* was a type of creature called a nimravid. In fact, at this point in history, there were no true cats yet, which is why *Dinictis* can't be classified with other well-known predators like *Smilodon populator* (see page 268).

HAVE YOU EVER HEARD THAT CATS ALWAYS LAND ON THEIR FEET? TRUE CATS WALK ON THEIR TOES AND ARE VERY AGILE, BUT BY STUDYING THEIR FOOT BONES, SCIENTISTS CAN TELL THAT *DINICTIS* WALKED ON FLAT FEET.

Dinictis had strong canine teeth that would have been useful for holding onto prey.

LIKE MODERN LARGE CATS, *DINICTIS* MAY HAVE BEEN AN AMBUSH HUNTER THAT STALKED ITS PREY BEFORE POUNCING.

HYAENODON GIGAS

AMONG THE EARLIEST MAJOR MAMMAL PREDATORS WERE THE CREODONTS—CARNIVORES LIKE *HYAENODON* THAT RAN ON ALL FOURS AND CUT THROUGH FLESH WITH SPECIALIZED CHEEK TEETH THAT SLID PAST EACH OTHER.

Hyaenodon would have lived in Europe, Asian, and North America, and somewhat resembled modern canines.

HYAENODON HAD A STRONG NECK AND A HEAVY HEAD FILLED WITH TEETH.

Like modern dogs, *Hyaenodon* would have used its mouth and teeth to grab onto food.

HYAENODON HAD SLENDER LIMBS THAT WOULD HAVE HELPED IT TO BE ACTIVE, BUT IT LIKELY WOULDN'T HAVE USED THOSE LIMBS TO PICK UP PREY.

Have you ever seen a dog digging a hole? *Hyaenodon* paws may have also been useful for digging into the ground to hunt animals that lived in burrows or holes.

HYAENODON HUNTED IN AN AMBUSH STYLE THAT'S ACTUALLY SOMEWHAT SIMILAR TO MODERN LARGE CATS. IT WOULD BRIEFLY PURSUE ITS PREY BEFORE POUNCING AND PUSHING ITS TARGET TO THE GROUND.

ARCHAEOTHERIUM MORTONI

YOU MIGHT PICTURE PIGS LIVING ON FARMS, BUT LONG BEFORE THEY WERE THE PIGPEN-LOVING CREATURES WE KNOW TODAY, THEY ROAMED THE WILD. SOME EVEN STILL DO, LIKE WILD BOAR, AND THEY'RE MUCH MORE INTIMIDATING THAN THE CUTE PIGLETS YOU MIGHT SEE ON A FARM VISIT. THIS PREHISTORIC PIGLIKE CREATURE WAS FIRST DISCOVERED IN 1850 AND WAS KNOWN TO LIVE IN NORTH AMERICA.

At the time, the habitat was largely occupied by early mammals like horses, leaving little competition except *Hyaenodon gigas* for predators like *Archaeotherium*.

ARCHAEOTHERIUM HAD WIDE CHEEKBONES AND JAWS THAT COULD OPEN WIDE AND CLOSE AROUND PREY EASILY.

With its large canine teeth, it would have easily been able to capture prey or pick up food from the ground.

DID YOU KNOW THAT MODERN PIGS ARE CONSIDERED TO BE SOME OF THE SMARTEST ANIMALS? THAT'S NOT TRUE OF THEIR PREHISTORIC ANCESTORS. ARCHAEOTHERIUM MAY NOT HAVE BEEN THE SMARTEST CREATURE AROUND, BUT IT LIKELY HAD A PRETTY KEEN SENSE OF SMELL THAT IT LIKELY USED TO HUNT. THIS ISN'T TOO UNLIKE MODERN PIGS, WHICH HAVE AN EXCELLENT SENSE OF SMELL.

By studying its skull, scientists can tell that *Archaeotherium* had forward-facing eyes that likely had good vision.

TITANIS WALLERI

PRONUNCIATION: TIE-tan-ISS

SIZE: About 8 feet (2.4 meters) tall

LIVED: 4.9 to 1.8 million years ago

PHYSICAL PROFILE: A large "terror bird" with small wings, strong legs, and a large, powerful beak

Giant, carnivorous birds evolved multiple times throughout prehistory, but the most impressive of all were surely the terror birds.

FLIGHTLESS BIRDS FIRST EVOLVED ABOUT 62 MILLION YEARS AGO AND WERE MAJOR PREDATORS UNTIL 2.5 MILLION YEARS AGO. ALTHOUGH THEY MOSTLY LIVED IN SOUTH AMERICA, ONE OF THE LAST—TITANIS—MADE IT TO NORTH AMERICA.

So how did it get there? After tens of millions of years of separation, South America became connected to North America at modern-day Panama about seven million years ago. This allowed animals like saber-toothed cats to move south, and South American creatures like *Titanis* to move north.

THIS BIG BIRD WAS NOT FRIENDLY. IT WOULD HAVE BEEN ABOUT 8 FEET (2.4 METERS) TALL, EQUIPPED WITH SHARP TALONS AND A STRONG BEAK.

TITANIS WAS SOMEWHAT OF AN ANCIENT EXPLORER, AND THE BIG BIRD MADE IT AS FAR AS FLORIDA.

Titanis fossils were first found in 1961 in the Santa Fe River in Florida.

MOST PEOPLE SCUBA DIVE TO SEE FISH, BUT AFTER THE FIRST *TITANIS* DISCOVERY, FLORIDA MUSEUM CREWS USED SCUBA GEAR TO SEARCH FOR FOSSILS IN THE SANTA FE RIVER, WHERE THEY RECOVERED SEVERAL *TITANIS* SPECIMENS.

If you want to see fossils of *Titanis* in real life, they're on public display in the fossil hall of the Florida Museum of Natural History.

PALAEOLOXODON NAMADICUS

PRONUNCIATION: PALE-ee-oh-LOCK-sa-dawn

SIZE: Up to 16 feet (4.8 meters) tall and 48,000 pounds (21,772 kilograms)

LIVED: About 24,000 years ago

PHYSICAL PROFILE: This ancestor of the elephant had two long, straight tusks.

This prehistoric mammal is part of a group of animals called Proboscidea and was related to mammoths and modern-day elephants.

This massive creature was both large and heavy, and scientists suspect that it may have been one of the largest mammals to ever walk the Earth!

SMILODON POPULATOR
PRONUNCIATION: SMAI-luh-DAWN

SIZE: About 7.5 feet (2 meters) long

LIVED: 13,000 to 10,000 years ago

PHYSICAL PROFILE: *Smilodon* had a body similar to a modern tiger with a massive jaw and saber-like canine teeth, and also a short, bobcat-like tail.

DON'T LET THE NICKNAME "TIGER" FOOL YOU— *SMILODON* ISN'T RELATED TO MODERN TIGERS. ALTHOUGH *SMILODON* LOOKS A LOT LIKE A MODERN BIG CAT, THERE'S NOT MUCH EVIDENCE THAT IT'S DIRECTLY RELATED TO ANY MODERN SPECIES OF CAT. THE ANCESTORS OF THE CATS WE KNOW DIDN'T APPEAR UNTIL A FEW MILLION YEARS LATER.

TRUE OR FALSE

1. T/F ARCHAEOTHERIUM MORTONI HAD A TERRIBLE SENSE OF SMELL AND NEEDED TO RELY ON OTHER SENSES WHEN HUNTING.

2. T/F *DINICTIS FELINA* WAS A SABER-TOOTHED TIGER.

3. T/F ALTHOUGH MOST OTHER TERROR BIRDS STAYED IN SOUTH AMERICA, *TITANIS WALLERI* FOSSILS HAVE BEEN FOUND IN NORTH AMERICA.

You might know this creature by its more common name, the saber-toothed tiger!

Can you guess where this creature got its nickname? Unsurprisingly, it came from its saber-like teeth! *Smilodon* had long, slender canine teeth like saber swords and were undoubtedly just as deadly.

Those teeth weren't just for show. *Smilodon* was a predator that could take down prey much larger than it was. It would have hunted massive mammals like prehistoric camels and bison that shared the same forest habitat.

Smilodon is one of the more well-known prehistoric creatures because scientists have found so many fossils in North and South America.